(continued)

Restructuring Schools for Linguistic Diversity,
Second Edition
OFELIA B. MIRAMONTES, ADEL NADEAU, & NANCY L. COMMINS

Words Were All We Had
MARÍA DE LA LUZ REYES, ED.

Urban Literacies
VALERIE KINLOCH, ED.

Bedtime Stories and Book Reports
CATHERINE COMPTON-LILLY & STUART GREENE, EDS.

Envisioning Knowledge
JUDITH A. LANGER

Envisioning Literature, Second Edition
JUDITH A. LANGER

Writing Assessment and the Revolution in
Digital Texts and Technologies
MICHAEL R. NEAL

Artifactual Literacies
KATE PAHL & JENNIFER ROWSELL

Educating Emergent Bilinguals
OFELIA GARCÍA & JO ANNE KLEIFGEN

(Re)Imagining Content-Area Literacy Instruction
RONI JO DRAPER, ED.

Change Is Gonna Come
PATRICIA A. EDWARDS, GWENDOLYN THOMPSON MCMILLON, &
JENNIFER D. TURNER

When Commas Meet Kryptonite
MICHAEL BITZ

Literacy Tools in the Classroom
RICHARD BEACH, GERALD CAMPANO, BRIAN EDMISTON,
& MELISSA BORGMANN

Harlem on Our Minds
VALERIE KINLOCH

Teaching the New Writing
ANNE HERRINGTON, KEVIN HODGSON, & CHARLES MORAN, EDS.

Critical Encounters in High School English, Second Edition
DEBORAH APPLEMAN

Children, Language, and Literacy
CELIA GENISHI & ANNE HAAS DYSON

Children's Language
JUDITH WELLS LINDFORS

"You Gotta BE the Book," Second Edition
JEFFREY D. WILHELM

No Quick Fix
RICHARD L. ALLINGTON & SEAN A. WALMSLEY, EDS.

Children's Literature and Learning
BARBARA A. LEHMAN

Storytime
LARWRENCE R. SIPE

Effective Instruction for Struggling Readers, K–6
BARBARA M. TAYLOR & JAMES E. YSSELDYKE, EDS.

The Effective Literacy Coach
ADRIAN RODGERS & EMILY M. RODGERS

Writing in Rhythm
MAISHA T. FISHER

Reading the Media
RENEE HOBBS

teachingmedialiteracy.com
RICHARD BEACH

What Was It Like?
LINDA J. RICE

Research on Composition
PETER SMAGORINSKY, ED.

The Vocabulary Book
MICHAEL F. GRAVES

Powerful Magic
NINA MIKKELSEN

New Literacies in Action
WILLIAM KIST

Teaching English Today
BARRIE R.C. BARRELL ET AL., EDS.

Bridging the Literacy Achievement Gap, 4–12
DOROTHY S. STRICKLAND & DONNA E. ALVERMANN, EDS.

Out of This World
HOLLY VIRGINIA BLACKFORD

Critical Passages
KRISTIN DOMBEK & SCOTT HERNDON

Making Race Visible
STUART GREENE & DAWN ABT-PERKINS, EDS.

The Child as Critic, Fourth Edition
GLENNA SLOAN

Room for Talk
REBEKAH FASSLER

Give Them Poetry!
GLENNA SLOAN

The Brothers and Sisters Learn to Write
ANNE HAAS DYSON

"Just Playing the Part"
CHRISTOPHER WORTHMAN

The Testing Trap
GEORGE HILLOCKS, JR.

Inquiry Into Meaning
EDWARD CHITTENDEN & TERRY SALINGER, WITH ANNE M. BUSSIS

"Why Don't They Learn English?"
LUCY TSE

Conversational Borderlands
BETSY RYMES

Inquiry-Based English Instruction
RICHARD BEACH & JAMIE MYERS

Transforming Talk into Text

Argument Writing,
Inquiry, and Discussion,
Grades 6–12

Thomas M. McCann

FOREWORD BY
GEORGE HILLOCKS, JR.

Teachers College, Columbia University
New York and London

NATIONAL WRITING PROJECT

National Writing Project
Berkeley, CA

Published simultaneously by Teachers College Press, 1234 Amsterdam Avenue, New York, NY 10027 and the National Writing Project, 2105 Bancroft Way, Berkeley, CA 94720-1042

The National Writing Project (NWP) is a nationwide network of educators working together to improve the teaching of writing in the nation's schools and in other settings. NWP provides high-quality professional development programs to teachers in a variety of disciplines and at all levels, from early childhood through university. Through its network of nearly 200 university-based sites, NWP develops the leadership, programs and research needed for teachers to help students become successful writers and learners.

Much of Chapter 3 originally appeared in McCann, T. M., D'Angelo, R., Hillocks, M., Galas, N., & Ryan, L. (2012). Exploring character through narrative, drama, and argument. *English Journal, 101*(6), 37–43. Copyright © 2012 by the National Council of Teachers of English. Reprinted with permission.

Library of Congress Cataloging-in-Publication Data is available at loc.gov

ISBN 978-0-8077-5588-4 (paper)
ISBN 978-0-8077-7331-4 (ebook)

Printed on acid-free paper
Manufactured in the United States of America

21 20 19 18 17 16 15 14   8 7 6 5 4 3 2 1

*This book is dedicated to the memory of
my old friend Larry Johannessen,
a great teacher, scholar, and collaborator.*

Contents

Foreword

In the fall of 1955, I began my quest for a teaching certificate in English when I attended the College of Wooster. The first requirement of the program was that we visit 24 to 30 classes in real public schools over 2 weeks. I observed again what I had always seen in schools: desks arranged in rows, teachers talking up front, and a high level of generalized boredom. Interestingly, at least to me, one class stood apart and became the foundation for what I was to learn over the next several years and has changed my life in ways I could not have imagined at the time.

Judging from the work of contemporary scholars (Goodlad, 1984; Hillocks, 2002; Nystrand, 1997), I'm willing to bet that if you walked about classrooms in a random sampling of schools today, you would see exactly the same kind of teaching that I witnessed in my early observation experience in 1955. Things are very slow to change. And though the scholars who study this teaching are nearly adamant in their advice to change, teachers ignore the encouragement.

When asked, teachers explain that they teach as they have always taught, the way they have been taught themselves, and the way they expect to teach into the future. When teachers claim to have discussion in their classrooms, what we observe is really recitation. I have even had the interesting experience of observing classrooms with nothing but teacher talk. In one of these the teacher informed me later in an interview the same day that the class had had quite a good discussion on this day. However, I had made notes of student contributions. I had only one indication of a student talking. He had come into class late and apologized for his tardiness. That was all. No other comments from students at all, and yet the teacher regarded the class as a "good discussion."

I suspect that there are two reasons for this failure. First, teachers are unfamiliar with specific means of instigating and maintaining an active discussion with a whole class. Even less familiar to them is small-group discussion, which many teachers claim "just doesn't work." Teachers often explain that they give students topics to discuss but the discussion falters and falls apart, setting students free on other conversations of interest to them but of no relevance to the class focus. Under such circumstances, we have learned, little or no learning takes place. Under these circumstances, small-group discussion does not work.

In this important book, Tom McCann has given us not only the admonition to change, but the details about what effective change must be and what it looks like, evidence that it works effectively, and details about how to bring it to pass. In this work, each activity leads to the next. A whole-class discussion prepares students for small-group discussions by catching their interests, revealing how to work with the questions that are set up, demonstrating how students can come to agreement even when they disagree, and helping them to learn how to summarize the results of their discussions. Any classroom discussion needs to begin with students' interest and/or experience so that they can participate early in the processes of learning. They need a topic or information that they can look at and think about and know something about so that they can express opinions and ideas.

But no one said that such teaching is an easy task. It is difficult, time-consuming, and energy depleting. It may be the most difficult thing you have ever tried in teaching if you have not already done it. It can be discouraging to the faint of heart. It can take many days if you make a mistake, and it doesn't always work as you had hoped. But when a classroom comes alive, I don't know the teacher who would ask for a better experience. I'm talking about the energetic exchange of ideas with children jumping out of their seats at times to express their ideas, to clarify a point, to agree or disagree with another student, and to enliven the entire class with their contributions. What I'm talking about is part of real honest-to-God learning of sometimes very difficult and complex concepts. It can generate enthusiasm for leaning that can last a lifetime. It has been the central ingredient of the joy I have lived through a lifetime. I wouldn't want to have lived without it. We should all thank Tom for bringing us this rich gift.

—George Hillocks, Jr.,
Professor Emeritus, University of Chicago

Preface:
Inquiry, Discussion, and Writing

A substantial body of research in the teaching of writing reveals that frequent purposeful interactions among peers, as part of the writing process, positively affects the quality of the writing that students produce. In reviews of experimental treatment studies (Graham & Perin, 2007a, 2007b?; Hillocks, 1984, 1986a), researchers report the effect size associated with instructional treatments that emphasize high levels of peer interaction and compare the results with the effect sizes associated with other treatments, concluding that discussion-dependent approaches benefit learners a great deal. Later research (e.g., Applebee & Langer, 2013; Juzwik, Borsheim-Black, Caughlan, & Heintz, 2013) affirms these earlier findings. For the teacher who relies on research to guide practice, the implication is that writing instruction should feature frequent peer interaction. The teacher might see the obvious correlation: Frequent peer interaction leads to higher-quality scores for students' writing. But for the teacher who tries to align instruction with research, practice might be a kind of act of faith, without the teacher really knowing why high levels of peer interaction would be important. What is missing from the research is a detailed probe into *what happens during peer interactions* that accounts for students developing highly elaborated, logical, and coherent compositions.

It is important that a theory of instruction drives what teachers do in practice. The expression of theory will benefit from a teacher knowing what it is about peer interactions that influences how the learners develop their writing. For me, the compelling question has been this: What occurs during purposeful peer interactions during writing instruction that accounts for the raised quality of written work that students produce? This is what I hope to show in this book.

TALK AND THE WRITING PROCESS

It is easy to assume that writing instruction has progressed significantly since Applebee's 1981 report, which revealed that teachers in secondary school by and large were assigning students writing tasks without much preparation and with reliance on comments on papers as the primary means of instruction. While more progressive process-oriented approaches have taken hold since the 1981 report, Applebee and Langer (2006, 2013) note that learners' frequent discussions are still not typical elements in the process of preparing to write.

INQUIRY AND DISCUSSION-BASED APPROACHES TO THE TEACHING OF WRITING

This book features a few experienced teachers who rely on discussion as a central element in the process of preparing students to write. The teachers' efforts to foster inquiry prompted much of the discussion. The reconstruction of some of the classroom discussions reveals students at work: expressing conclusions, citing examples and other data as support for claims, interpreting data, questioning or challenging claims and warrants, offering exceptions, and evaluating the merits of multiple perspectives. These are procedures that seem obviously connected to the kind of writing that students are preparing to draft, and seem to transfer to the examples of writing re-created in this book. The coding of transcripts reveals something about the distinct function of each discussion in a series of discussions. The coding also reveals a purposeful sequence across a set of discussions. In interviews, students identify how they compose and note their awareness of the functions that the formal and informal discussions serve.

The teachers featured in this book have planned for discussions as essential parts of an inquiry sequence. The teachers' actions as discussion facilitators and their reflections during interviews reveal their dialogic moves and the thinking behind their practice. The views of the teachers in action and their reflections allow for a summary of the moves of a skillful inquiry and discussion planner and facilitator.

ORGANIZATION OF THE BOOK

At the beginning of this book, I argue that students learn to write by talking to one another. Even when students are the less-active players in conversations, authentic discussions immerse the learners in procedures that become important when students write. For the teachers featured in this book, the discussions are part of a broader inquiry effort that connects talking, researching, writing, and reading. An introduction to inquiry prepares the reader for the work of teachers who plan strategically and who facilitate each of their discussions as a purposeful stage in an inquiry process.

Most of the chapters of this book illustrate teachers at work, from 5th grade through high school. Sets of transcripts reconstruct the talk in the classroom. The transcripts reveal patterns of talk across a set of lessons. Interviews with teachers reveal their intentions for each discussion. Samples of students' writing show the effect that the discussions appear to have on the compositions that the learners produce; and in interviews, the students report how discussions support their effort to produce academic writing.

Chapter 7 generalizes about how teachers construct inquiry-based activities that rely on frequent discussions. The chapter also describes a teacher's purposeful moves in fostering inquiry and facilitating authentic discussions in an expanding sequence that emerges from a compelling problem that invites shared investigation and that connects discussions, writing, and reading across several weeks of instruction and learning.

SERVING A DIALOGIC SHIFT

In *Writing in the Dialogical Classroom* (National Council of Teachers of English [NCTE], 2011), Bob Fecho argues for dialogical writing, which involves the use of various kinds of texts and engages students in their writing as a form of discovering identity. From a theoretical perspective, Fecho argues for the teaching of writing in a classroom that privileges students' talk. In order for teachers to move into a dialogic stance, they will need to know why students' involvement in discussions might be important and also what a skilled teacher does to foster inquiry, to plan and facilitate individual discussions, and to connect a purposeful sequence of discussions to prepare writers and deepen understanding of critical issues. I expect that this book will serve these ends.

Acknowledgments

Several important researchers influenced the conception and execution of this book. I am particularly indebted to my friend, teacher, and mentor George Hillocks, Jr., who has long emphasized the importance of learners' classroom interactions, and the teacher's role in carefully planning for purposeful interactions. I also owe much to the groundbreaking work of Martin Nystrand, who has reported how little authentic discussion occurs in schools and why we should care. I acknowledge also the influence of Mary M. Juzwik, Carlin Borsheim-Black, Samantha Caughlan, and Anne Heintz, who have explored ways to change the classroom landscape to make it more dialogic.

Several friends, exceptional teachers, and gifted writers have shown time and again the promise of inquiry-based approaches to instruction. The work of Peter Smagorinsky, Elizabeth Kahn, Larry Johannessen, Carolyn Calhoun Walter, Michael W. Smith, Jeffrey Wilhelm, and Steve Gevinson has showcased the many options for fostering inquiry and infusing instruction with meaningful discussion.

I am particularly grateful to several distinguished teachers who have helped me to think about the work of teachers and to appreciate the careful preparation that goes into the work they do every day. These teachers include Becky D'Angelo, Nancy Galas, Laura Ryan, Mary Greska, Chanelle Savich, Joseph M. Flanagan, Dawn Forde, Andy Bouque, Jennifer Roloff Welch, Melina Probst, and Ashley Mitrovic. Their work has served me as inspiration, and they have been generous with their time in helping me to understand how the careful planning for discussion impacts learning and students' positive experiences in the classroom. Other accomplished teachers and school leaders have served as examples for how it is possible to expand English language arts instruction so that it moves beyond simple targets and narrow assessments. These teachers and leaders include Suzanne Bell, Patti Dalton, Jackie Komos, Drew Herrmann, Jim Trottier, Kim Gwizdala, Melanie Kleimola, Laura Pfau, Danielle Johnson, Nicole Cox, Nicole Boudreau Smith, Barbara Alvarez, Andrea Cobbett, and Mary Joyce Howard.

Many of my colleagues who are committed to teacher preparation have affirmed that their efforts at colleges and universities to prepare teachers offer hope to influence emerging teachers to work in inquiry-based, dialogic ways. These committed educators include Dianne Chambers, Paula Ressler, John Knapp, Judy Pokorny, Susan Callahan, Brad Peters, and Laura Bird.

Tracy Stephens was an enormous help with the research process and took care of a great deal of drudgery that was essential to completing the project. Tracy also read early drafts of some chapters and provided helpful insights to make the chapters better.

I am indebted, as always, to Pam McCann for patient sufferance through the research and development of this book. Pam has been generous in reading and commenting on drafts and in encouraging the work over several years.

I am grateful to the editors and production staff at Teachers College Press. I am especially indebted to Emily Spangler, who saw promise in this project from the beginning and has contributed generously to its development to a more refined expression than its coarse beginnings would have suggested.

CHAPTER 1

Learning to Write by Talking

WRITERS AT WORK TOGETHER

A look into one class of 10th-graders reveals students busily talking about significant critical issues. Mr. Minton,* their teacher, introduced a specific family that wants to protect its safety and security, but also recognizes that some attempts might compromise their sense of privacy. In preparing students to write about a compelling current issue, Mr. Minton organized discussion as a role-playing activity, with students assuming different positions related to questions about surveillance and privacy protections. Here is a bit of the large-group exchange:

Ashton (role of parent): We have to monitor the kids a lot so that we know they are always safe.

Jackie (role of adolescent child): It (monitoring) is OK in moderation, like we are going to the park and there is a safety issue. But not at home. It goes too far when you don't have privacy.

Sammie (role of adolescent child): The stress of the constant monitoring is going to make me want to strike out and do something radical, like become a drug addict.

Sharon (role of parent): We want to protect our children. The safety of the children is important. We need to know they are safe all the time.

Cameron (role of police officer): Parents have control of their kids until they are 18, so parents will do what they have to do to keep them safe.

Jackie (role of adolescent child): We are already safe at home without being monitored by video surveillance. Don't we have some basic human rights?

Garret (role of "Big Data" collector): Why are the kids nervous if they have nothing to hide?

Sammie (role of adolescent child): And why are the parents upset about someone watching *them* when they feel justified in watching *us*?

Connie (role of child): Parents should trust us so that we can learn from our independence.

---

*The names of the teachers and the students represented in this book are all pseudonyms, many of which have been selected by the participants.

While the students are, in a sense, playing, they are involved in some serious talk about the balance between the pursuit of safety and security and the need for privacy. The participants in the conversation question assumptions, express values, point out inconsistencies, and defend positions. Mr. Minton set the process in motion, but stepped back to allow the students to have a mature conversation about tough issues. Mr. Minton intended that the class discussions, in their many forms, would prepare students for writing an argument for a course of action that would both secure safety and protect privacy. Many sources (Applebee & Langer, 2013; Juzwik et al., 2013; Nystrand, 1997) note that this reliance on purposeful peer interactions as part of the preparation for writing is uncommon in schools. But Mr. Minton believes that students learn to write by talking, as well as by writing—a position supported by research and an understanding that has guided my practice as a teacher of writing. In this book I hope to show what happens when students talk to one another. I expect that the discussions that I have reproduced, the students' related writing, the students' commentary on their writing, and the teachers' reflections on their practice will reveal the many ways in which students' frequent interactions support their inquiry and writing. I also will illustrate the moves that teachers make to promote dialogue and reveal the thinking behind teachers' planning and classroom decisions.

As I expect to show below, a substantial body of research reveals that students' frequent participation in authentic discussions has a strong impact on the quality of the writing that these students produce. The difficulty for teachers, perhaps, is seeing how the trends revealed by the research translate into practice in the classroom. A close look at what teachers do to foster classroom dialogue and an examination of students' involvement in various kinds of discussions will suggest what dialogic practice might look like and why it is worth pursuing.

THE WAY WE WERE

In a 1981 research report for NCTE, Arthur Applebee observed that an assign-and-assess model of instruction was the dominant mode for the teaching of writing in secondary schools. He reported, "In the observational studies, the amount of time devoted to prewriting activities averaged just over three minutes. That included everything from the time the teacher began introducing the topic until the first student began to write" (p. 74). But even the 3 minutes between assignment and composing were not devoted to substantive preparation for the task. Applebee goes on to report that "those three minutes were spent writing the essay topic on the board, or passing out and reading through a dittoed assignment sheet, followed by student questions about task dimensions: 'How long does it have to be?' 'Can I write in pencil?' 'Do I have to do this?'" (p. 74).

This picture of common practices in secondary schools in 1981 reveals that many teachers assumed that students already knew what was expected of them and readily could produce writing when prompted to do so. The description also suggests that many teachers placed the instructional emphasis on the correctives they provided after students had turned in their writing. The apparent understanding among teachers was that there was value in students making attempts at writing and in teachers telling the students what they had done wrong so that they would avoid the same mistakes in the future. Of course, many teachers have come to understand that, for many reasons, the assign-and-assess model doesn't work very well. Hillocks (1982) reveals that teachers' comments on student-produced work have little effect on improving the quality of students' writing.

LEARNING TO WRITE BY WRITING

Much work in the field of the teaching of writing has been done since the Applebee report. In light of the influence of Emig (1971), Murray (2003), Graves (1983), Macrorie (1986, 1996), Daniels and Zemelman (1988), Atwell (1998), and others, it would be reasonable to expect that practices in schools have changed significantly since 1981. The good news from Applebee and Langer's later reports (2006, 2013) is that writing instruction has changed in schools. The most important of these changes include the teaching of writing as a process, with attention to prewriting activities, and the movement from initial planning to drafting to revising and editing. More recent classroom practices take advantage of conferencing with students as they work through the composing process, and, sometimes, interaction among peers at various stages in the process.

These reformed approaches to the teaching of writing suggest that writers learn to write by writing. Certainly the approaches sponsored by Macrorie (1986), Graves (1983), and Atwell (1998) emphasize such practices as frequent journal writing as a means for students to explore ideas, plan, develop, and elaborate. Teachers facilitate exploratory and supportive conferences with students as a key element in the composing process.

LEARNING TO WRITE BY TALKING

Another body of research suggests that as students learn to write, they benefit from talking with their peers as well as from writing. The meta-analyses of Hillocks (1984, 1986a) and Graham and Perin (2007a, 2007b) suggest that purposeful talk among developing writers is an important part of the process of learning composing procedures and of refining specific compositions. Graham and Perin (2007b) organize their meta-analysis categories around "key elements" of instruction. They note that one of the most powerful elements is collaborative writing. They define *collaborative writing* in this way: "Collaborative writing involves developing instructional arrangements whereby adolescents work together to plan, draft, revise, and edit their compositions" (2007b, p. 16). In his meta-analysis, Hillocks compared the relative effects of six instructional approaches, or foci, and reported that the inquiry-based approach had by far the most positive impact on the quality of students' writing. Hillocks considered an approach to be an *inquiry* approach when "it presented students with sets of data (or occasionally required them to find data) *and* when it initiated activities designed to help students develop skills or strategies for dealing with the data in order to say or write something about it" (1986a, p. 211, emphasis in original). In working in an inquiry mode, students work with one another to grapple with problems, and they have access to relevant data to support their efforts. The frequent interactions immerse students in the processes that are important to composing (e.g., defining, narrating, analyzing, arguing, etc.). The inquiry approach then combines two of the key elements that Graham and Perin report as offering great promise for students' development as writers: learning context-specific strategies for problem solving and composing, and collaborating with peers.

In his discussion of the studies considered for inclusion of his meta-analysis, Hillocks (1986a) comments on two notable experimental treatment studies: Troyka (1974) and McCleary (1979). These two studies reveal the significant impact of students' purposeful talking with one another as an element in the composing process and in the course of learning to write.

Troyka (1974) worked with students in a community college. As a part of their writing instruction, the students participated in a series of simulations that required role playing. The students worked with data, analyzed a problem, and deliberated with other students about the merits and shortcomings of different approaches and perspectives to the problem. Each simulation required a different type of written response (e.g., the examination of different vehicles available for a taxicab company to purchase required a comparison/contrast analysis; a nation's budget crisis required an argument as to the appropriate policy for cutting or increasing department budgets and balancing the overall budget). Hillocks reports that the gains for the learners in the Troyka study exceeded by far the gains in the other studies that he examined. As a classroom teacher looking at the Troyka study, I wanted to know what happened in her classroom to account for such a positive effect on learners. The approach in the Troyka study had these features: (1) The students worked toward solving a particular problem; (2) the teachers provided students with relevant data that they could use in their analysis; (3) the students recognized a specific context for addressing the problem; (4) the students worked with particular strategies for making sense of the data and addressing the problem; and (5) the activities relied on purposeful peer interaction.

McCleary (1979) also worked with students in a community college. In his study, McCleary sought to measure the comparative effects that teaching two different systems of formal logic had on the students' production of "logical writing." Three control classes were taught no formal logic. McCleary reported that there was no significant difference in the results across the treatment groups. However, *all* of the groups of students, no matter what the instructional treatment, made significant gains in the quality of their writing during the course of a semester. All the treatments in the McCleary study, whether the students received formal training in logic or not, involved students' deliberating about specific scenarios that raised questions about ethical behavior. As the students discussed and debated with one another about the merits of different responses to the ethical dilemma, they apparently developed strategies for thinking logically and arguing their positions. The McCleary study reveals that regardless of the model of logic emphasized, all groups made significant gains. So it seems that the important factor is not which model of logic a teacher emphasizes, or whether a teacher teaches a formal model of logic at all. Instead, it appears that the important element was the interaction among the students as they grappled with the ethics problems represented in scenarios.

So, have we learned anything from these early studies to guide our practice as writers? Applebee and Langer's 2006 study offers some good news about the state of writing instruction in middle and high schools. The authors note that from 1988 to 2002, there was an increase in the amount of writing students were asked to complete, students had greater access to technology to support their writing, and teachers increasingly had participated in related professional development—all factors that the researchers connect with increases in the quality of students' writing. At the same time, while students have relatively frequent occasions to write, they "seem not to be given assignments requiring writing of any significant length or complexity. This is of particular concern for the college-bound students who will be expected to write even longer papers when they begin their college course work, as well as for those entering better-paying jobs with higher literacy demands in the workforce" (Applebee & Langer, 2006, p. 12). The authors report also that teachers typically approach writing as a process: "By 1998, the emphasis on process instruction was consistent across subgroups of students defined by race/ethnicity and by eligibility for free or reduced-price lunch" (p. 23). At the same time, referring to practices in Grades 8 and 12, Applebee and Langer report that by 2006, "strategies requiring interaction with others were somewhat less frequent at both grades" (p. 23). "Less frequent" in this case means that fewer than a third of the students reported that interaction among peers was a common practice. So there is good news about teaching writing as a process, but disappointing news that teachers seldom structure purposeful interactions among peers as a distinct element in the composing process.

It is curious that teachers seem to have accepted the idea that composing is a process and that the teaching of writing requires more than assigning and assessing, but at the same time many process-oriented approaches do not take advantage of the power of opportunities for students to talk about the problems at the core of specific writing tasks and about their attempts to compose. The studies by Hillocks (1984, 1986a), McCleary (1979), Troyka (1974), Graham and Perin (2007a, 2007b), and Applebee and Langer (2013) underscore the important role that students' interaction with one another plays in helping students to develop command of specific thinking and composing procedures and in advancing the quality of students' written compositions. The too frequent absence of purposeful peer interaction as part of the composing process invites a closer examination of what happens when students interact as part of a structured process, and a consideration of the advantages that derive from including purposeful student conversations as a key element in writing instruction. I illustrate below the role that discussions play in the writing process. In later chapters I will reveal in detail how students explore and refine thinking and composing procedures as they interact with peers in a variety of discussion forums.

EXAMPLES OF A "STRUCTURED PROCESS" APPROACH

In a *structured process* approach to teaching composition, a teacher plans carefully for the experiences and supports that will help students to write highly elaborated, organized, and coherent compositions (Applebee, 1986; Smagorinsky, Johannessen, Kahn, & McCann, 2010). Students benefit from purposeful interaction with one another at various stages during the composing process. During the planning stage, students benefit from working with one another to explore ideas and refine their plans. As they develop their work, they can share with one another what they have composed and benefit from having an authentic audience to react to what they have written. The following example illustrates how the interaction with classmates allows students to grapple with problems, explore possibilities, identify parameters, and generate ideas for composing a story. Through the process, students discover something about the procedures that are necessary for composing a narrative. In turn, they can apply these procedures in new situations when they are invited to tell a story again.

AN INQUIRY INTO NARRATIVE

In this sample activity, a 5th-grade teacher, Ms. Wieczorek, presents a class with a set of paired sentences, offered as the beginning and end sentences for a series of episodes that will be woven together as one larger story. The writing that students produce in these circumstances is relatively informal, and the instructional focus is on helping students to develop a means–ends strategy for composing a narrative.

Ms. Wieczorek begins the process for this kind of collaborative narrative by explaining that the students will be writing a story together and noting the purpose for such a composition: to learn about conventional narrative structures, to anticipate plot in their subsequent reading, to recognize a common pattern of narrative, or to develop procedures for producing a fairly complex narrative (McCann, D'Angelo, Hillocks, Galas, & Ryan, 2012). While each group of students will focus on one episode, all of the students will need to be aware of the tendencies of the multiple episodes in order to fit an individual episode into the whole. In practice, then, the teacher shows students the prescribed beginning and ending sentences for all of the episodes. In the process, it would be worthwhile for the teacher to pose reflective questions aloud and note the implications of the episode and the demands for resolutions.

Ms. Wieczorek introduces the collaborative story by exposing the students to the complete set of sentences. As she shares the beginning and end sentences for each episode, she asks the students to suggest what the sentences suggest about the substance of the episode.

THE PLAYGROUND BULLY: A STORY IN SIX EPISODES

EPISODE 1

Beginning Sentence: When Shelley, Byron, and Keith parked their bikes and walked onto the playground, they saw the same sort of scene that had terrorized them at John L. Lewis School since August.

End Sentence: As the boy lifted himself from the ground, muddy saliva oozed from the corner of his mouth, and Dillon jangled the loose change in his mud-caked fist.

EPISODE 2

Beginning Sentence: At lunch that day, Dillon leaned over their table and hissed, "I'll see you three after school."

End Sentence: They pulled their bikes into Shelley's yard, panting softly and marveling about how they had outrun their menace.

EPISODE 3

Beginning Sentence: The next morning, the three friends stopped their bikes at the far end of the playground and puzzled how they would get to the bike rack and slip into school past Dillon, who stood with his arms crossed at the main entrance of the school.

End Sentence: They walked safely down the hall for now, but they knew that they could not get into school the same way every day.

EPISODE 4

Beginning Sentence: When Shelley emerged the next morning from her grandmother's basement apartment, she held in her hand the simple gift her grandmother had given her, claiming that she would appreciate its value more and more every day.

End Sentence: They had escaped his grasp once again, and recognized that this common object had liberated them from their tormentor.

EPISODE 5

Beginning Sentence: Two of Dillon's friends sat on the bike rack at Lewis School, apparently waiting for the three to arrive.

End Sentence: Safely inside their classroom, they realized how lucky they were this time that help had arrived, but they knew that help would not always be there.

EPISODE 6

Beginning Sentence: As the three friends mounted their bikes and began to peddle away, Dillon and his two buddies stepped into their path.

End Sentence: When it was all over, everyone appreciated that what Shelley, Byron, and Keith had done was difficult; and they realized that life at John L. Lewis Elementary School would never be the same.

Here is an example of the interchange between the students and the teacher as they studied the sentences from episode 1:

Ms. Wieczorek: The first sentence says, "When Shelley, Byron, and Keith parked their bikes and walked onto the playground, they saw the same sort of scene that had terrorized them at John L. Lewis School since

August." The last sentence says, "As the boy lifted himself from the ground, muddy saliva oozed from the corner of his mouth, and Dillon jangled the loose change in his mud-caked fist." What must have happened between the action suggested by the first sentence and the action suggested by the last sentence?

Tyler: I think that he pushed him down and he got all muddy.

Maggie: One of those guys—Shelley, Byron, and Keith—got hit.

Ms. Wieczorek: I am wondering why the writer didn't use one of their names. It just says, "the boy." And who did the hitting?

Madison: It's that guy Dillon. I think what happened is that he hit someone and took away the kid's lunch money.

Ms. Wieczorek: How did that happen?

Maggie: I know, I know. He, Dillon, told this kid to give him his lunch money, but he didn't want to. So he made him give him the money.

Ms. Wieczorek: What makes you think Dillon took the boy's money?

Maggie: He's jingling the money in his hand.

Ms. Wieczorek: The boy, the victim, has muddy saliva coming from his mouth. How did mud get into his mouth?

Tyler: Dillon probably hit him when his hand was muddy. It says, "his mud-caked fist."

May: It says his "fist," like he was fighting.

Ms. Wieczorek: I see there are other hands up. But we have a lot of ideas, and we'll leave it up to the team to decide.

As Ms. Wieczorek introduces the narrative task, the students begin to invent the story, which involves evaluating the possibilities and trying out details. The lesson transitioned then to small-group planning. The following exchange among a small group of students reveals the kind of thinking in which they engage as they explore options for completing the episode. The structure of the activity calls for them to rely on a *means–end strategy* for composing; that is, they recognize an apparent goal—to make the beginning sentence connect logically to the end sentence—and they have to honor the constraints represented by those sentences to guide them in developing the body of the episode in a logical way for the sake of the episode itself and in order to connect to the other episodes that their classmates are writing.

Tyler: I'd like it to be a good situation if they go back to school, that they stood up to Dillon. If it's bad, they stood up to Dillon and they became the bullies themselves. They go down the path and one of them falls off his bike, . . .

Lauren: So, he falls off of his bike?

Tyler: They came to a stop real fast in front of the three boys.

Lauren: Do we know their names?

Tyler: I don't know. I picture them on the Prairie Path, and these guys jump out in front of them and they stand up to the bullies and then become bullies themselves.

Lauren: But how would everyone appreciate them? It says that everyone appreciated them.

Tyler: Yeah. We have to figure that out. Cam, what would you say for dialogue?

Cam: Like, "Oh, no, not these guys again."

Tyler: He could say, "We have some unfinished business." And he could remember about some bad thing that happened.

Lauren: Or he says something mean about someone.

Tyler: Cam, what could cause this big of a conversation?

Cam: They feel bad about being bullies, and they change.

Lauren: Would they say, "Get out of my way"?

Cam: Or a teacher could be coming down the path and helps them.

Tyler: Somehow they have to do something that's not violent but difficult to do.

Lauren: They could stand up to Dillon and say that they are tired of this and they are not going to put up with it any more. I like stories when the bully realizes that what he did was wrong.

Cam: That sounds like a good idea. He could be sorry and become friends with them.

Tyler: That way, the school will never be the same.

It is fairly easy for an English teacher to recognize that the narrative that students produce in this situation will imitate to a certain extent the cycle of the hero story. In addition to giving students some experience in composing a narrative, the effect of the exposure to the combined six episodes is that the class as a whole has produced a narrative that is similar in plot and theme to the romance of the hero that they might encounter in works like *The Hobbit* or *The Wizard of Earthsea* or *The Odyssey*. For many students, this will be an advantage in helping them to read a complex narrative. The experience also helps students to anticipate themes and critical questions about a more mature narrative, as they draw from their own knowledge and sense of values to judge what might happen and what the characters should do.

In this situation, with students learning procedures for generating a narrative, the teacher's emphasis in assessment should be on the collaborative process, recognizing that the students' working together to produce a story will help them to develop some composing procedures that they can apply on other occasions. In other words, the teacher monitors whether students have command of basic procedures for narration: sequencing action; describing characters, setting, and events in sufficient detail; handling dialogue; and connecting an episode logically with other episodes in the broader story. In many ways, the stories that students produce are unpredictable, and it would be inappropriate to set a narrow quality standard. The function of the assessment is to see evidence of command of procedures that students later can apply independently.

AN INQUIRY INTO ARGUMENT

The next example illustrates how students can become immersed in the thinking and composing procedures necessary to generate logical arguments and to analyze the comparative advantages among several possible courses of action. In order to create the dynamic for peer interaction, the teacher introduces a commonplace problem that the students can recognize and care about. Students initially work together to try to imagine a particular point of view in regard to a conflict. As they proceed, they share with one another the multiple perspectives.

After the sequence of discussions, the teacher prompts a particular kind of writing—in this case, an argument to a specific authority or to a principal player in a human drama to advise that reader about a policy question: How should disputed lottery winnings be distributed? The prompt would invoke a quality standard familiar to the students, identify a particular audience, and align directly with the procedures that students practice during discussions; that is, frame a problem, state a position, support a recommendation through a series of connected arguments, and recognize and evaluate competing points of view. If a teacher's or a peer's comments about a student's writing during a draft stage are going to be of any use, those comments need to connect with the standard already familiar to the learners. The task represented by the prompt should align with the problem-solving activities during discussions and not diverge from the classroom work that preceded the writing.

The Big-Time Lotto—What Is Important?

Background: Five friends who worked together for the W.E. Burrough Excavation Company regularly pooled their money to purchase lottery tickets each week. They took turns each month in accepting the responsibility to purchase the tickets. Everyone pitched in $5 each week to be able to buy a total of 25 tickets. They thought that buying the tickets in bulk would improve their odds for winning, and they agreed that they would divide the proceeds of any prize. Last winter they won several free tickets, and in May they won and evenly divided $250. In early summer something remarkable happened that tested their friendship.

One of the friends, Tony, did not show up for work on a Monday morning. When the construction manager called Tony's home, his wife reported that he was incapacitated with a backache. In fact, she said, his back problems were chronic, causing him to seek the help of a medical specialist in another state. She said that Tony regretted that he would not be able to return to work. He was sorry about the inconvenience, but his health came first.

At first, the other friends—Allie, Chris, Pat, and Sal—thought nothing about another weekend without lottery winnings. That was typical. They were disappointed, however, that their friend would not return to work. After a time, Allie became suspicious about Tony's disappearance, so Allie contacted the State Lottery Office, where she learned that Tony had won the $28 million jackpot. This meant that, after taxes, each member of the lottery-playing group would take away about $2.3 million in winnings.

Problem: When Allie and the other co-workers pursued their claim with the State Lottery Office, they learned that Tony claimed that the winning ticket was one that he had purchased *separately* from the group purchase, although he did not make photocopies of the separate tickets to share the group numbers with his co-workers. The central question now is this: *Should Tony share his winnings with the co-workers with whom he had been playing the lottery?* This central question connects with other related questions:

- Is there a precedent or a lottery rule that could force Tony to share the winnings?
- What principles should apply in determining the distribution of the money?
- To what extent should the circumstances in each co-worker's life influence the distribution?
- To what extent has Tony violated principles of friendship and honesty in keeping the winnings secret from his former co-workers?
- If Tony is forced to share the winnings, should he also be punished in some way? What principles would guide the decision to punish and determine the extent of the punishment?

Related Information: The following information should help you in thinking about the case and preparing for discussion. The information appears below in two forms: (1) guidelines from the State Lottery Office to advise players about safeguards for Group Play, and (2) links to related articles that reveal other persons in similar circumstances.

State Lottery Office—Guidelines for "Group Play"

Often groups of friends or family members enjoy playing the State Lottery together. This means that several persons will contribute, but one leader actually purchases and holds the tickets. Often the responsibility for purchasing the tickets and managing the record-keeping falls to a different person each week or with each Lottery drawing. Timely purchases and careful record-keeping are essential. Everyone who wants to join Group Play needs to contribute toward the purchase of tickets in a timely way in order to have a fair claim on any winnings. It seems appropriate that each member of the group should seek information about the purchases so that the process is transparent and reduces the chance for dispute and animosity.

Each group could set up its own rules, but it seems reasonable that each person receive a share of the winnings that is in proportion to the contribution; that is, a $1.00 contribution = 1 share of the winnings, a $2.00 contribution means 2 shares of the winnings, and so on. We recommend that each group member sign a paper that documents commitment and contribution. We recommend also that the group leader make photocopies of the group tickets so that everyone can enjoy the excitement of the numbers being drawn, and to avoid disputed claims.

Remember that only a single player can claim winnings of less than $600. If a group wins a substantial jackpot, all the group members will enter a partnership that is subject to state and federal taxes.

Related Reading: Other lottery players have found themselves in similar circumstances. You can research related news stories on your own or consult the following articles:

"Woman sits out office Powerball pool—and coworkers win," NBCNews.com, March 27, 2013

"Lottery-winning hairdresser says she can prove her case," *USA Today*, April 10, 2013

Directions for Discussing the Case: As with many difficult situations we may find ourselves in, it is useful to start by imagining the thinking from the several perspectives in the case. The class will discuss the central question in three phases.

1. *Small-group preparation:* With two or three other members of your class, prepare an argument from the point of view of a single character. See the descriptions of the characters below. You might not agree with this character, but you will want to understand the character's thinking. Your argument should attend to the following questions:

- How should the lottery winnings be distributed among the members of the group?

- What evidence ("facts" about past practice and current behavior) can you offer to support your conclusion?

- What rules apply to the evidence to allow you to draw your conclusion about the distribution of the money (e.g., past practice, State Lottery Guidelines, principles of friendship, fairness, decency, etc.)?

- How do other analogous (similar or related) cases help us in thinking about the current situation?

Be sure to take notes as you prepare so that you are ready with a coherent argument when the entire class discusses the case.

2. *The Lottery Office Forum:* Enter into a discussion with the whole class to listen to the arguments of others and to contribute the argument of your assigned character. If everyone is to arrive at a deeper understanding through negotiation, it is important that everyone have a chance to speak without interruption. It is also critical that you be able connect your contribution by citing the position of someone else with whom you either agree or disagree to some extent.

3. *Be yourself:* Although you have imagined the case from an assigned point of view, you might not agree with this point of view, or you may have changed your thinking after you have had a chance to hear other thinkers. In this stage of discussion, you will abandon your assigned role and think about the case from your own point of view: How should the winnings be distributed? What should happen to Tony? To what extent is there merit to the arguments of the various characters involved in the case?

Points of View: While there are perhaps two distinct sides to the case (Tony vs. his co-workers), there can be several perspectives that inform the ultimate decision. With other members of your group, imagine how one of the characters is experiencing the circumstances and develop the argument that the character would make in a forum to negotiate a possible settlement.

Tony: Tony believes that he has done nothing wrong and claims he is having medical problems, which explain his quick and "convenient" disappearance. While he did purchase tickets for the group, he bought his own tickets separately. He judges that he has honestly claimed winnings on his own personal ticket.

Allie: Allie has always been suspicious of Tony. Allie feels as though she has to execute a plan of revenge against Tony and that he needs to be penalized for what he did to the group. When she was a group leader, Allie always made photocopies of the lottery tickets to share with every member of the group. She judges that as a rule of play, Tony should have done the same, in order to avoid difficult situations like the current one. It is hard to judge the truth in the situation if someone is not able to document the distinction between group play and personal play.

Chris: Chris always tries to see the best in people. He has his reasonable doubts about Tony, but does believe that it is possible that Tony bought his own tickets apart from the group tickets. Chris does think that each group member should receive a token amount, not the entire amount, but a good-faith portion, just in case Tony did steal the group's winning lottery ticket.

Sal: Sal remembers that at one time Tony said to him that if either he or Sal acquired a winning lottery ticket, the two of them should just split the winnings and not share them with the rest of the group. Sal claims he would have never gone along with it. Sal believes that this earlier conversation reveals that Tony has an inclination toward cheating.

Pat: Pat currently faces very difficult times. Pat has a child with leukemia, requiring a lot of medical attention. Pat is in danger of losing his home due to all the medical bills. Pat is prepared to argue that each group member should get a share of the winnings in proportion to his or her need. Pat's need seems to be greatest, so his family should get the greatest portion.

Lottery Official: The State Lottery official admits that there are no strict rules about Group Play, but there are published guidelines. The official can recite those guidelines and offer that the current group could have avoided conflict if they had taken some simple steps to guarantee trust and transparency. The official knows that each group member has a responsibility to promote trust.

The following exchange draws from several discussions among high school students. Their interchanges reveal their immersion into several processes: They attempt to generate reasons to support their position. They try to imagine the opposition to their position in order to construct counter-arguments. In the process, they clarify the position they are trying to defend, and they summarize their position in order to be able to represent it to others. The various thinkers assume roles, even though the teacher has not assigned them specific responsibilities: Someone keeps the group on task and clarifies what they should be doing; another student inadvertently helps the group to imagine an opposing perspective; someone else elaborates; and someone summarizes.

Sylvia: All right, what are we saying?

Ivan: We're Pat, right?

Doug: This guy [Tony] is sleazy. He shouldn't get any money.

Ivan: But that's not what Pat would say. He doesn't want to keep all of the money from Tony, but he wants a big amount.

Doug: Then Tony should get the smallest amount.

Freda: Pat has the most need. He's going to argue that the more need you have, the more money you should get.

Sylvia: But that's not what they agreed to, I mean, in the beginning.

Doug: They agreed to share, but Tony didn't. And he ran off and lied to everyone.

Ivan: So he should get some smaller amount. But, like, Pat is arguing that he should get the most. His kid is sick and he has a lot of bills, medical bills.

Freda: Yeah. Now that Tony has . . . violated the earlier agreement, then the money doesn't have to be divided evenly. Pat has the greatest need and he should get the most.

Sylvia: OK, so what are we saying, then?

Doug: We are arguing that everyone should get an amount according to his need, and Pat needs the most.

Sylvia: So, what are our reasons?

Doug: His kid is sick. He has lots of bills. Tony cheated, so he should get
    the least. *Fairness* is not the same as *equal*. What we are saying is that
    what's *fair* depends on what someone *needs*.

After the small-group preparation, the students in the class experienced
the neighborhood forum, where they offered their competing perspectives
and questioned and challenged one another to consider exceptions and to
provide further support for their positions. In the end, through their interactions with one another, the students could recognize that there wasn't just
one viable perspective on the controversy. Their thinking shifted to consider
the most advantageous course of action, in light of the merits and disadvantages associated with each point of view.

The class discussion exposed students to multiple perspectives that they
would have to represent in some way in a fully developed argument about
the case. In discussing the same case, a teacher with an interest in adding a
multimedia element to this approach could ask students to use a wiki environment to state their positions and review those of others. When students
post their positions on a wiki, other students can draw from this online
writing in order to refine their own thinking and to develop summaries that
they can evaluate in their own compositions.

THE VALUE OF TALK: A VYGOTSKIAN PERSPECTIVE

These two sample activities take advantage of students working together
and interacting on many levels. Experience over decades of teaching and
my examination of student-produced work suggest to me that as emerging
writers, students benefit greatly from their interactions with others. From a
research and theoretical base, I draw support from Vygotsky.

First, Vygotsky (1986) reminds us that learning is social. This does not
mean simply that students should engage in a lot of small-group activities,
although that would be better than having few or no opportunities to work
collaboratively with classmates. Learners are products of their social milieu,
and with a community of learners they can confront vexing problems that
they are well prepared to tackle with the support of the adult teacher and
their peers.

> Unlike the development of instincts, thinking and behavior of adolescents are
> prompted not from within but from without, by the social milieu. The tasks
> with which society confronts the adolescent as he enters the cultural, profes-
> sional, and civic world of adults undoubtedly become an important factor in

the emergence of conceptual thinking. If the milieu presents no such task to the adolescent, makes no new demands on him, and does not stimulate his intellect by providing a sequence of new goals, his thinking fails to reach the highest stages, or reaches them with great delay. (p. 108)

In purposeful small-group work and during authentic whole-class discussions, several processes are at play, as demonstrated in the brief interchanges above: The contributors identify and evaluate options; they elaborate and defend assertions in the face of challenges; they support the positions and suggestions they approve, and question the offerings that they don't embrace; they evaluate the quality of evidence and the speaker's interpretations of it; and they consider the exceptions to generalizations. These efforts would be less likely without the interaction with peers, which creates the conditions that raise doubt and challenge previously held positions. In the face of the interactions with others, it is unlikely that the learner will remain static, but will move along in an attempt to reconcile inconsistencies and resolve doubt. Again, Vygotsky (1978) reminds us of the importance of the interaction with others:

We propose that an essential feature of learning is that it creates a zone of proximal development; that is, learning awakens a variety of internal developmental processes that are able to operate only when the child is interacting with people in his environment in cooperation with his peers. Once these processes are internalized they become part of the child's independent developmental achievement. (p. 90)

WHAT MAKES AN INSTRUCTIONAL ACTIVITY WORTHWHILE?

Of course, it is not enough to move students into classroom activities and to get them to talk. Perhaps we can all recall occasions as students and as teachers when the talk in the classroom seemed unfocused, meandering, and pointless. Newmann, Marks, and Gamoran (1996) caution us against the danger of thinking of activity involving peer interaction as an end in itself: "Reform efforts focused on active learning may lead down an illusory path where student participation in activities can become an end in itself, regardless of the intellectual quality of students' work" (p. 281). In their thoughtful reaction to the danger of embracing activity as an end in itself, Newmann et al. recommend three general criteria for defining the intellectual quality of the activities in which we hope students will engage.

First, they suggest that the activity should help students to construct or produce knowledge or meaning, as opposed to reproducing it. The simple contrast is a recitation-based classroom where students reproduce information or recite positions that the teacher will endorse, as opposed to a discussion-based classroom where students engage together into the exploration of ideas while they practice the skills and procedures that can transfer to their writing.

Next, Newmann et al. encourage *disciplined inquiry*. Classroom activities that foster disciplined inquiry would activate relevant prior knowledge, help students to develop in-depth understanding of a problem or of concepts central to a discipline, and require elaborated communication. Again, in classrooms where students remain passive, or simply recite responses to questions that have prespecified answers, students will not participate in exchanges that require qualifications, elaborations, nuance, details, extended narratives, justifications, and analogies. In contrast, well-constructed, inquiry-based classroom activities create a dynamic situation in which students have to practice these communication procedures.

Finally, Newmann et al. advise that another standard for the intellectual quality of classroom activities is that they have value beyond school. This seems consistent with Langer's (2001) idea of *generative learning*. If students complete an activity that seems to have limited application outside a classroom and is executed solely for the purpose of checking off a class requirement, they are unlikely to have learned procedures for thinking, judging, or composing from which they can draw in order to accomplish similar tasks and build on their learning in the future.

PLANNING FOR PURPOSEFUL TALK

How does a teacher design the kind of learning activities that will take advantage of students working together in a purposeful way as an element in their composing process? Chapters 2–6 illustrate the format and use of several inquiry-focused, discussion-based activities, while Chapter 7 describes at length the process of designing such activities. I offer here a brief summary of the process.

The design of an instructional activity that aligns with significant goals and engages learners in a social process of developing and practicing procedures for thinking and composing will follow a careful task analysis of the kind of writing that a teacher expects students to be able to produce. The teacher also must assess what students already know, in order to build on their prior knowledge and to target areas that students have yet to develop.

As a rule, students will engage enthusiastically in problem solving, as long as the problem is not a baffling conundrum and is one that they can recognize as significant to their own lives. The subject of the activity is important. Generally, problems set in schools, or involving young people as characters, resonate with adolescents. Students also engage with perennial problems, like conflicts with authority, working out friendships, deciding questions of equity or fairness or justice, and exploring the tension between personal liberty and obligations to a group or to authority. These subjects appear repeatedly as issues in literature and show up daily in the news and in other popular media.

It is not enough to design an activity that casts a problem at students. They need to be able to access the relevant information that will help them in making decisions and working out the problem. The teacher who designs an engaging activity will plan for accessing relevant information, will provide for the preparation for discussion, and will structure the appropriate forums for discussion, including opportunities that extend the interaction through social media or other online platforms. The phases of independent preparation, work in small groups, and large-group discussion precede subsequent composing stages, when students plan, draft, revise, and edit. The work with peers and with the teacher can support each of these stages.

Part of the task analysis involves a teacher's judgment about how much information the learners will need in order to engage in the procedures involved in inquiry and problem solving. Perhaps a teacher will judge that, for the moment, the students need practice in interpreting information such as photos or other visual images, brief texts, testimonies, or summaries of simple statistics. It would be easy enough for a teacher to supply such data sets for use in the classroom. In other instances, especially after students have mastered some basics of interpreting data, the teacher can build in a stage when students find information to support their thinking. In any case, the teacher needs to know the students well and needs to keep in mind the instructional goals and the students' current readiness to reach the targeted outcomes.

SITUATED IN A BIG CONVERSATION

Of course, thinking about writing as a social activity involves more than directing students to work in groups. In a broader sense, when students write, especially when they write arguments, they are participating in a broad conversation. If they are writing about policy questions related to *justice*, *fairness*, *personal liberty*, or *societal obligations*, they are participating in a conversation that has extended for thousands of years. In the most immediate sense, the writer will reveal an awareness of the conversation that has occurred in the classroom. More broadly, the writer might bring in the thoughts of other authorities who have wrestled with the same problems and have contributed their thoughts to the literature.

It would be reasonable to expect that young writers will recognize other authorities and opposing points of view as part of the process of framing the problem they are discussing and as a means for evaluating their own thoughts. An awareness of other thinkers helps the writer to frame a problem for the reader to consider and prompts elaboration.

TALK AND WRITING THAT FOSTER A DEMOCRATIC CLASSROOM

The teaching of writing as a social process that necessarily involves frequent interactions among peers will be part of a larger effort to help students to experience what it means to live in a democratic society where the decisions and actions of one person affect others, and where the individual reflects on the effects those actions have on others. The process of learning to write well through experiences that involve frequent interaction among peers cannot be haphazard, but should follow a purposeful structure that respects the dignity of the participants, even when situations seem competitive. Juzwik et al. (2013) suggest approaches to fostering a supportive environment for discussion. Classroom discourse should proceed rationally and civilly, if teachers are to promote involvement and foster complex thinking that honors a variety of perspectives in some way. Teachers can set a standard for group interactions, or work with a class to derive the norms for groupwork and whole-class discussions. These expressed norms are useful for helping students to become aware of how the way that they contribute, or resist contributing, affects their classmates. Groups can rely on the established norms to assess themselves and report to the teacher how the groups are functioning. These reports and the teacher's observations can guide adjustments to group membership and to the procedures for large-group forums.

This insistence on civility during discussions certainly protects the dignity of all contributors and helps students to feel more secure in their participation. But insistence on civility is more than a matter of being polite. If the classroom discourse is to support inquiry, then the interchanges must elevate above shouting matches and put-downs in the style of the worst of talk radio and staged discussion dramas on television. Nussbaum (1997) observes:

> In order to foster a democracy that is reflective and deliberative, rather than simply a marketplace of competing interest groups, a democracy that genuinely takes thought for the common good, we must produce citizens who have the Socratic capacity to reason about their beliefs. It is not good for democracy

when people vote on the basis of sentiments they have absorbed from talk-radio and have never questioned. This failure to think critically produces a democracy in which people talk at one another but never have a genuine dialogue. In such an atmosphere bad arguments pass for good arguments, and prejudice can all too easily masquerade as reason. To unmask prejudice and to secure justice, we need argument, an essential tool of civic freedom. (p. 19)

In the same spirit, Meier (1995) insists that frequent purposeful engagement among peers promotes democratic ideals by involving learners in practices that are essentially democratic: "The habits conducive to free inquiry don't just happen with age and maturity. They take root slowly" (p. 81). To support inquiry that involves critical thinking and prepares learners for subsequent writing, a teacher would not just provide opportunities for students to talk to one another. The teachers whose work I highlight in this book have thought about the strategic linking of one discussion to another as part of an ongoing conversation and investigation. Nussbaum and Meier remind us that active, frequent engagement over an extended period of time in meaningful discussions not only promotes the learning of the relevant procedures for a particular writing task and other literacy learning goals, but also fosters an environment of tolerance, critical thinking, and democratic spirit.

An approach to writing instruction that focuses on "free inquiry," as Meier calls it, invites a closer examination of *inquiry* as a process that involves problem solving, critical thinking, and frequent interactions among peers. The next chapter takes a closer look at *inquiry*. My vision of inquiry involves the kind of peer interaction that will involve learners in procedures important for critical judgments, analysis, and argument. Subsequent chapters look closely at what learners do as they engage with one another in small groups and in whole-class discussions as exploratory talk that precedes attempts at producing elaborated and refined responses to critical issues.

CHAPTER 2

An Introduction to Inquiry

TEMPLATES, INTRODUCTIONS, AND INQUIRY

In reviewing the instructional units that my undergraduate students created as part of their work in a methods class, I noticed a few lessons that directed students to produce compositions that followed a rigid template, including the requirement to begin the introduction to the essay with an "attention getter." When I questioned the wisdom of insisting that students conform to these conventions, the authors of these lessons cited their cooperating teachers, the curriculum of the school, or the school's adopted textbook as authorization for both the five-paragraph template and the "attention getter" introduction. Despite the instruction and models to which the prospective teachers had been exposed during their preparation at the university, it appears that when they entered schools for clinical experiences, they followed instructional practices that emphasized reading and writing algorithms, and sometimes conformed to self-imposed scripts. There are ways for beginning teachers to approach mentor teachers about alternatives to the established scripts, and all teachers may have greater curriculum autonomy than seems apparent (see, e.g., McCann, 2011).

For years, researchers and education commentators have cautioned against reliance on such rigid templates because they prompt formulaic responses and superficial thinking. It is curious that the five-paragraph essay formula stubbornly persists. Johnson, Thompson, Smagorinsky, and Fry (2003) trace the pressures that influence teachers to promote the form. In part, local school leaders promote a writing formula that they perceive as aligning with the evaluation standard associated with state assessments of writing. Hillocks (2002) notes that the training materials and the scoring rubric for such assessments often honor the five-paragraph essay. In addition, teachers often impose their own restraints by mimicking the kind of instruction they received as students and by imitating the practices of more experienced colleagues.

There is nothing new about cautioning against teaching students to rely on the five-paragraph theme formula, but the adoption of the Common Core State Standards (CCSS) and attention to conceptions of "college and career readiness" make it urgent to think of teaching and learning in a different way; and the kind of writing that aligns with the Standards will defy the use of simple formulas. Consider, for example, the standard that calls for students to be able to "develop claim(s) and counterclaims fairly and thoroughly, supplying the most relevant evidence for each while pointing out the strengths and limitations of both in a manner that anticipates the audience's knowledge level, concerns, values, and possible biases" (CCSS Initiative, 2010, p. 64). The standard and the accompanying sample compositions (CCSS ELA Appendix C) suggest an instructional target that requires, among other demands, an awareness of a complex intellectual conversation that includes various voices that contribute to the writer's thinking about the central issues for argument. Such complexity does not lend itself to the three points that make up the body of a five-paragraph essay, a form that suggests the writer can advance a proposition without regard to competing perspectives.

I am not so much interested here in railing against the five-paragraph theme, but I want to argue for exposing students to more mature and adaptable alternatives that both align more closely with what academic writers actually do, and serve learners better in developing command of the kinds of procedures that the Common Core State Standards promote. I suggest also that if students are to write in mature and elaborated ways, their writing is likely to be the product of inquiry processes, and not the result of plugging content into a template.

I will define *inquiry* in greater detail later in this chapter, but I offer briefly here, after Dewey (1938) and consistent with Hillocks (1986a), that inquiry is a process that begins with the recognition of some problem or area of doubt and moves systematically to seek at least tentative answers, solutions, or clarifications. The inquiry process inevitably requires access to information and consultation with other thinkers, and should include an awareness of the procedures that the thinker followed in order to arrive at conclusions.

The Common Core State Standards set as targets that by the end of high school, students will be able to write arguments, "informative/explanatory texts," and narratives. Furthermore, the standards suggest that these forms of writing are not rigid genres, but are forms of expression built on research and adapted to the goals of a given situation and to an understanding of the characteristics and needs of an audience. The Standards call for teaching students to be able to produce a variety of different kinds of writing, all of which are clear, coherent, organized, concise, and precise. As a teacher of composition at a university, I recognize the Standards as desirable goals for the kind of writing my students should be able to produce. The question is, How do we get there? I know this: We won't get there simply by listing the desirable characteristics and telling the students to produce something that exhibits these traits.

I focus here on teaching students to write *arguments*, which hold a "special place" in the Standards. Writing in schools appears under a lot of different labels—for example, exposition, reports, thesis papers, analysis papers, and so on—but all of these forms of written expression rely on *argument* in the sense that the Standards suggests: focusing attention on a general proposition, advancing the proposition through related claims, supporting claims through citing relevant and accurate information, explaining what the information means and how it connects to claims, identifying opposing positions and evaluating their merits. Hillocks (2011) notes that there are various kinds of arguments and distinguishes the kind of thinking that each situation requires. Smagorinsky, Johannessen, Kahn, and McCann (2010, 2011) also review various kinds of arguments and suggest a sequence of instructional activities that engage learners in the kind of procedures that are appropriate for each argument. For each kind of argument, the writer will need to think logically and analytically, and certainly composition teachers would expect the writer to advance arguments that are organized, coherent, and precise in the use of language.

In "articulation" meetings (i.e., meetings for the purposes of discussing common issues and aligning efforts toward a shared goal) that I have attended with participants from high schools, community colleges, and universities, the discussion of the Standards has come around to the idea of "college readiness" as an outcome of teaching toward the Standards. Of course, it is hard to agree on what "college readiness" means. I think that if I were to ask 10 different university professors what the phrase means, I would hear 10 different but definitive answers. But the Common Core State Standards Initiative (2010) cites Gerald Graff in underscoring the important place that argument holds in schools and in readying candidates for the intellectual life of the university (p. 24). Graff (2004) would be an appropriate scholar from whom to seek support. He insists boldly that "summarizing and making arguments is the name of the game in academia" (p. 3). This observation encapsulates a lot of what I see at the university: Students are expected to listen to others and to read complex texts in order to summarize the arguments of others, if we think of *arguments* as the logical development of thought, something along the lines that the Standards target for writing. In addition, students should be able to advance their own arguments, especially in the context of the arguments that the students have identified and associated with other thinkers. This idea of being able to summarize the arguments of others and advance one's own arguments, situated in the accurate representation of an ongoing debate or deliberation or inquiry, is both essential to what students should learn by the end of 12th grade, and a tall order for the teachers who will prepare learners to meet the Standards and be "college ready."

If students are going to "develop claim(s) and counterclaims fairly and thoroughly, supplying the most relevant evidence . . ." (CCSS Initiative, 2010, p. 64), they will need to be aware of the swirl of arguments that surround a proposition in order to spot the specific area of doubt that needs to be investigated and illuminated for the sake of the writer and for an audience that can be convinced to read the writer's arguments. Again, this isn't going to happen by offering students a rigid template for argument, even if the template is accompanied by several model compositions and by detailed rubrics that express a quality standard. While writing prompts such as the ones illustrated in this book are likely to frame a problem and suggest a quality standard for students' writing, both the problem and the standard should connect to previous discussions from which they were derived. This is distinct from offering a boilerplate model and a long rubric that are supposed to structure whatever content the learners seek to fit into the framework. These more rigid efforts emphasize exposure to an abstract and static form, and neglect to involve learners in the procedures of inquiry that help students to draw and support conclusions as they judge the merits of competing views.

ENTRY INTO INQUIRY

The point of entry into inquiry is the raising of doubt about subjects and issues that the learners care about. This does not mean that students will be interested in tackling only the fleeting issues from their contemporary world, like the relative merits of various popular musicians, the esteem accorded the fashion judgments of their peers, or the quality of food offered in the cafeteria. Instead, preadolescent and adolescent learners will energetically tackle the same sort of questions about equality, justice, responsibility, freedom, compassion, love, and loyalty that Shakespeare and thousands of other writers have grappled with for generations. At least, this has been my experience in working with students from 5th grade through college. Stern (1994) notes that finding the focus of inquiry is not pandering to students' passing fancies, but is a "cocreative" process (p. 5) that depends much on the teacher's understanding of students and respect for their existing knowledge and interests. Smith, Wilhelm, and Fredricksen (2012) recognize the influence of George Hillocks (1986b) in inviting us to pay attention to an "inquiry square" that illustrates how inquiry taps into both declarative and procedural knowledge (p. 21). Gevinson, Hammond, and Thompson (2006) make the compelling case that students' involvement with inquiries into significant problems have the potential for changing their experience in school and in the community, perhaps protecting them from descent into violence.

Williams (2004) notes that one of the problems that university students have in writing academic essays is that they have difficulty in framing the problem that will be the focus of the discussion in the paper. Imagine an essay about gun control beginning with this "attention getter": "Did you ever wonder what it would be like to experience the thrill of firing a gun?" Or, the "hook" into a critical analysis about *Hamlet* might offer this: "While the public might worry about violence in the media today, consider how many dead bodies lie about the stage by the end of the fifth act of *Hamlet*." Perhaps the interests of some readers would be sufficiently piqued to read on for a bit, but these invitations to longer discussions are hardly compelling. These two examples do not represent what academic writers do, and I judge that they do not reveal evidence of "college readiness." In contrast, Williams suggests that academic writers acknowledge the reader's understanding of the subject but introduce a problem, or an area of *doubt*, one so significant that it is worth the reader's cognitive investment to read through the balance of the essay.

In order to frame the significant problem, the writer must be aware of the existing field of knowledge or the ongoing conversation about the subject. For example, the writer might acknowledge that all citizens care about gun violence that slaughters children in schools and innocent people attending a theater or waiting in a bus shelter. The problem represented in heated debates focuses on the question of policy—on what *action* we should take to curb violence and protect the innocent. The *action* to take to curb gun violence, not the appalling *fact* of gun violence, is the area of doubt, the focus of attention for inquiry and discussion. To get to the point where writers can frame this problem, they would have to be aware—through reading, viewing, and listening, and especially through dialogue with others—of the relevant information and the competing arguments in regard to gun violence.

One function of a literature review for a thesis or dissertation is to demonstrate that a scan of the existing research and commentary about a subject reveals a significant area of doubt, which becomes the focus for the current research. The writer will have some hypothesis in mind, but the question that emerges from the area of doubt drives the inquiry, defines the methods of investigation, and underscores the significance of the findings. The written report conforms to some established conventions, but it takes its form as a *product of inquiry*. The emphasis on honoring a template suggests that a necessary and authoritative form exists and it is the writer's obligation to find the stuff to fill it up with. The process perhaps supports "career readiness" if the learner sought a rare career that involved primarily algorithmic thinking—the reliance on a set formula to complete a task; but I would not call this *inquiry* in the sense of an honest effort to learn and to illuminate an area of significant doubt for the writer and for the readers.

INQUIRY DEFINED

I have used the term *inquiry* several times. The use of the term invites a detailed definition, since there are various conceptions of what inquiry is. I offer here a definition by noting some key characteristics of inquiry and by providing an illustration of an inquiry process that leads to elaborated writing along the lines that the Common Core State Standards set as a target. One authority about inquiry and inquiry-based instruction is John Dewey. In *Logic: The Theory of Inquiry*, Dewey (1938) defines *inquiry* in this way: "Inquiry is the controlled or directed transformation of an indeterminate situation into one that is so determinate in its constituent distinctions and relations as to convert the elements of the original situation into a unified whole" (pp. 104–105). I understand Dewey to mean that inquiry begins with the recognition of an area of doubt, an "indeterminate situation." This recognition leads to the expression of a question or questions (i.e., a *problem*) that set off an investigation or the purposeful seeking of a solution to resolve the doubt, at least by arriving at tentative conclusions and by shedding some light on areas that previously had been dim. The investigation relies on reasoning and the command of techniques, operations, or procedures that will support illumination. For Dewey, the inquiry process might result in something more "determinate." At the same time, inquiry into one question often triggers other questions and an inquiry cycle continues. This is all very abstract; in practice for the purposes of classroom instruction, inquiry would have the features described below.

FEATURES OF INQUIRY

A Compelling Problem: A meaningful, central problem guides investigation, and the problem has no prespecified answers. The central problem is embedded in a specific and recognizable context. This is to say that a problem would not involve a broadly abstract concept like *freedom of expression*, but seek to judge the value suggested by this freedom when it collides with other interests, like *security* or *privacy* or *dignity*. The problem is likely to involve specific characters with specific interests in a specific situation. If a class of students were to investigate an area of doubt, they would likely consider the following questions:

- When, where, and why has the problem occurred?
- What are the constraints or specifications? All problems have complications, often setting parameters for action, which means that a problem-solver does not have unlimited options for solving the problem.
- How is the problem significant?
- What questions do you need to address as part of your investigation?

Access to Data: The thinkers have the means to access the data necessary to allow them to pose significant questions and to work on the problem. In some instances, it would be appropriate for a teacher to provide a data set to support inquiry; in other instances, the teacher might plan for a stage in the process for students to access information on their own, including data in the form of literary texts.

Procedures for Investigation: Students engage in the thinking strategies necessary to work on the problem (i.e., they develop and/or engage in procedures). In many cases, a teacher will have to model in some way how a mature thinker would proceed: in posing questions, in accessing information, in analyzing data, in evaluating competing points of view, in anticipating effects of proposed actions, etc.

Peer Interactions: Essential to the investigation are the opportunities for the students to interact in order to apply or practice the procedures for investigation:

- To build data sets, especially by tapping into the knowledge distributed among peers
- To develop and practice thinking strategies: e.g., arguing, defining, comparing, contrasting, analyzing, synthesizing, judging, etc.
- To foster respect for diversity of thought
- To promote habits of mind: remaining open to new possibilities, connecting the new problem to prior knowledge, persisting, reflecting on procedures, etc.

Report of Conclusions: The investigation leads to a related product or performance: e.g., a piece of writing, an oral report, a media presentation. Although the product might appear as an end point in an investigation, it also might identify additional areas of doubt and suggest other lines of inquiry.

Transfer and Application: There is a reasonable potential for students to apply the current learning to new contexts. If participation in the current inquiry has taught students some of the skills associated with inquiry (e.g., framing a problem, consulting a variety of sources, evaluating competing positions, summarizing and assessing individual arguments, synthesizing information, drawing from several sources to support a claim or proposition, interpreting and evaluating information, formulating arguments), then the learners should be able to apply the same skills in new situations, especially if the process includes a reflection stage that fosters an awareness of procedures.

PROBLEMS THAT RESONATE WITH LEARNERS

For the teacher planning instruction, posing problems that learners find compelling and that become the focus that drives inquiry and leads to elaborated writing will depend a great deal on knowing who the learners are. If a teacher is going to introduce doubt in a way that will grab students and join them together in shared inquiry, then the teacher will need to know the learners and the subject of the inquiry well. To introduce a problem that will invite students to devote their energies to grapple with complex texts and ideas and to engage with one another in a collaborative investigative process, the problems can't be esoteric questions that happen to be the teacher's pet interests. The problems have to resonate with the learners, to the degree that learners can see the problems touching their lives. Consider the contrast shown in Table 2.1.

I suggest that your garden variety middle school or high school student is not likely to imagine what the problems on the left are all about, even with some frontloading on the part of the teacher. But the questions in the right-hand column represent problems that students grapple with from day to day and that are also perennial problems that writers have represented and explored for centuries. I recognize, of course, that it is hard to say with confidence that certain problems will have universal appeal. The compelling nature of a problem will depend on the specific instructional context, which includes the nature of the learners and the issues and situations within their

Table 2.1. Selecting a Focus for Inquiry

Of Narrow Interest to Most Adolescent Learners	More Compelling to Most Adolescent Learners
Should the Army Corps of Engineers continue to maintain the Old River Control Project in order to channel the waters of the Mississippi River through New Orleans?	Must you obey your parents and other authorities all the time?
To what extent should we regulate financial institutions so that they do not endanger the economy as a whole through exotic and risky investment strategies?	To what extent are we obligated to help our fellow human beings?
How can we change practices in farming and family consumption in order to suppress the growth of algae in Lake Erie?	Should your neighbors regulate your behavior in any way, even when your behavior is likely to be destructive to you and members of your family?

community. I can well imagine that 10th-graders living in Morgantown, LA, might find the problem about the Old River Control Project quite compelling, because the destruction of the dam might mean that the residents of Morgantown could be swept into the Gulf of Mexico. But outside of this region of the country, the problem is going to seem less immediate and perhaps hard to imagine. How a teacher successfully frames a problem, then, will depend a good deal on knowing the learners whom the teacher wants to invite into the inquiry.

In order for learners to invest themselves in an inquiry process, the teacher will need to help them frame the problems at the heart of the investigation. It will not be enough to suggest problems as topics or titles, like *identity, justice, courage,* or *freedom.* It may not be enough to frame the problems as questions. Instead, students need to capture a strong sense of a problem through their consideration of an immediate, recognizable, and illustrative situation.

INQUIRY IN ACTION

I offer the case below as an example of a learning activity that can serve as an introduction to thinking about critical questions associated with texts commonly taught in high school: *1984, Fahrenheit 451, Brave New World, The Giver,* and *The Hunger Games.* The case represents competing values and interests, making it a debatable situation and an appropriate focus for inquiry. The teacher helps to frame the problem, but learners can contribute their own questions to guide the inquiry. The inquiry process relies on accessing information from a variety of sources, including texts and the students themselves. The process of formulating and expressing a position about the problem necessarily involves students in interacting with one another to develop the procedures necessary for forming critical judgments and for writing a fully developed response. In short, the students' involvement in the inquiry prepares them to meet the following standards, to name a few targets for 11th and 12th grades:

- *Write Arguments:* Write arguments to support claims in an analysis of substantive topics or texts, using valid reasoning and relevant and sufficient evidence.
- *Write Explanations:* Write informative/explanatory texts to examine and convey complex ideas, concepts, and information clearly and accurately through the effective selection, organization, and analysis of content.
- *Research a Problem:* Conduct short as well as more sustained research projects to answer a question (including a self-generated

question) or solve a problem; narrow or broaden the inquiry when appropriate; synthesize multiple sources on the subject, demonstrating understanding of the subject under investigation.

- *Read Complex Texts:* Integrate and evaluate multiple sources of information presented in different media or formats (e.g., visually, quantitatively), as well as in words, in order to address a question or solve a problem.
- *Discuss Complex Ideas:* Initiate and participate effectively in a range of collaborative discussions (one-on-one, in groups, and teacher-led) with diverse partners on Grades 11–12 topics, texts, and issues, building on others' ideas and expressing their own clearly and persuasively.

The language for the learning targets listed above comes from the Common Core State Standards. They are not important targets simply because a committee constructed, endorsed, and published them. If Graff is accurate in his claim that "summarizing and making arguments is the name of the game in academia" (2004, p. 3) then college-bound students will need to command these proficiencies in order to flourish in their college classrooms. But these are also key tools for functioning in a career and for living responsibly as a member of a community.

The following case offers an example of an instructional activity that initiates inquiry that involves extended oral discourse, elaborated writing, and connected readings. Some skillful teachers can initiate inquiry by posing a provocative question or citing a current news story. Cases such as the following, which derives from a variety of news stories and offers details and complications, have helped me to stimulate inquiry with groups of adolescents.

A SAMPLE CASE: THE PARENTS ARE WATCHING

When the Casto family recently visited a huge amusement park in Florida, the family had the option of purchasing global positioning system (GPS) wristbands for each of the children—Jackie, age 14; Connie, age 12; and Florence, age 10. With the use of a cell phone, each parent could spot the precise location of each child at all times. The wristbands gave Mr. and Ms. Casto some peace of mind, because they could allow the children a bit of freedom while still being able to track where each family member was at any time. When the children complained about wearing the wristbands, the parents responded, "This gives you *more* freedom, because you won't have to stay in our presence every minute that you are in the park."

The family enjoyed a safe and relatively entertaining visit to the park. Mr. and Ms. Casto appreciated the power of the wristbands so much that they decided to continue with their own version at home. They gave each child a cell phone on which they had loaded an app called "Find Me Now." The parents insisted that the children keep the phones with them at all times. From each parent's phone someone could spot the exact location of each child at any moment. If Florence was late for her ride to Taekwondo class, the parent could track her at the local convenience store. If Jackie was at the skate park when he was supposed to be home cleaning the cellar, there was no alibi. If Connie was cruising the mall, the parent could spot her at the cheap jewelry kiosk.

But the "Find Me Now" app was just the beginning. Mr. and Ms. Casto installed video cameras throughout their home so that from anywhere they could monitor home activities on their smart phones, tablets, and laptops. They could see if Connie was neglecting her Chinese studies, if Jackie was heating pizza puffs in the microwave before dinner, and if Florence was chewing her nails. Nowhere could the children escape their parents' care and attention.

It is hard to escape the watchful eye of other adults, as 14-year-old Jackie learned at school this year. Not only are there video cameras in hallways and outside of school, but this year teachers have taken to tracking online whether students are completing their assigned reading of e-books, and determining the students' level of "engagement" with the reading.

At the same time, Mr. Casto is careful to turn off his location on his smart phone so that others cannot monitor his behavior. And Ms. Casto resents the fact that Google, Amazon, Pinterest, and other online services track her searches and purchases so that vendors can profile her interests and specifically target her with ads that align with her profile. Both Mr. and Ms. Casto find it a disturbing intrusion when local municipalities install cameras at intersections and outside of businesses to watch them. They also know that if the local police want to track their movements for any reason, a police officer can secretly install a GPS sensor on their car. It is as if someone is watching them almost every moment of the day. These parents make a distinction between the security that they want to provide for their own family and the apparent intrusion into their own private lives by businesses and possibly by government.

Problem: While we all might be interested in privacy, we are also invested in our own security and the security of the people we love. We might be interested in protecting our private lives, but we also want convenience and often see a benefit in having others serve our interests and needs. The current situation with the Casto family invites us to propose a balance that honors our simultaneous interests in privacy, security, and convenience.

Questions: With other members of your class, prepare responses to the following questions, both from your own point of view and from the view of an assigned character:

- To what extent should Mr. and Ms. Casto monitor the actions of their children through electronic "surveillance"?

- To what extent should businesses and government entities be allowed to monitor the behavior of community members as they use phones, tablets, and computers to search and to purchase?
- What dangers do you see in the electronic monitoring of children and adults?
- What dangers do you anticipate if electronic monitoring and data collection and sharing escalate in the future?

Testimonials: In order to develop a full understanding of the problem, you will benefit from thinking about it from the points of view of the various people who are affected. What opinions would the following people offer about the fairness and wisdom of the almost constant monitoring of the behavior of law-abiding residents of their community? To begin, you and the other members of your small group should prepare a reaction from the point of view of an assigned character.

- Mr. Sammie Casto, father
- Ms. Adele Casto, mother
- Mr. Pat Roy, a representative from Data R Us, a company that collects personal data obtained from various online search tools and social networking sites
- Jackie Casto, age 14
- Connie Casto, age 12
- Florence Casto, age 10
- Captain Emily LaTargo, commander of the local police district

Additional Reading: How do current events stories inform our thinking about the issues with which the Casto family have been grappling? Before the class meets again, read at least two news articles about data collection/sharing, privacy rights, and security needs, and be prepared to summarize what you have read. Your summaries should contribute to our understanding of the problems. Here are some possibilities:

"Keeping Loved Ones on the Grid," *New York Times*, October 25, 2012. Online.

"Would You Put a Tracking Device on Your Child?" *New York Times*, Motherlode blog, October 23, 2012. Online.

"Mapping, and Sharing, the Consumer Genome," *New York Times*, June 16, 2012. Online.

"Private Snoops Find GPS Trail Legal to Follow," *New York Times*, January 28, 2012. Online.

"Supreme Court: Warrants needed in GPS tracking," *The Washington Post*, January 23, 2012. Online.

"War Evolves With Drones, Some Tiny as Bugs," *New York Times*, June 19, 2011. Online.

"Teacher Knows if You've Done the E-Reading," *New York Times*, April 8, 2013. Online.

STUDENTS IN ACTION:
WORKING WITH THE CASE

In using the case above, a teacher is likely to introduce the problem by summarizing the issues and noting how they are likely to connect with subsequent readings. The discussion is likely to involve several stages: (1) introducing the problem and reviewing the logistics involved in inquiring, (2) initiating and managing small-group work, (3) sharing observations and arguments across all groups, (4) reading related news articles and sharing what the articles contribute to the discussion, (5) modeling some components of a written response, and (6) following through with stages for composing a written response.

The transcript below reveals students' engagement in a large-group discussion. The discussion involves a class of 10th-graders and reveals the kind of exchanges that occur during an inquiry process. The students' talk in a large-group format shows their sense that the case represents vital questions for the conduct and quality of their lives in the future. Their involvement with the issues of the case immerses them in various processes (e.g., supporting assertions, evaluating the positions of others, responding to challenges, etc.) that become important for producing a written response to the situation.

Mr. Minton: Remember that this discussion is part of our larger consideration about how we respond to authority. Do we always have to obey authority? Does authority sometimes become too intrusive? How do we respond when we think authority is too intrusive? You are going to be assuming a role in a simulated meeting, so move your desks to form a circle. . . . Let's begin by hearing from someone in the business of collecting data.

Garret (role of "Big Data" collector): Our interest is in finding out what your interests are so that we can let you know about products and stuff that you might need. It really makes it easier for you.

Ashton (role of parent): We have to monitor the kids a lot so that we know they are always safe.

Jackie (role of adolescent child): It [monitoring] is OK in moderation, like we are going to the park and there is a safety issue. But not at home. It goes too far when you don't have privacy.

Sammie (role of adolescent child): The stress of the constant monitoring is going to make me want to strike out and do something radical, like become a drug addict.

Sharon (role of parent): We want to protect our children. The safety of the children is important. We need to know they are safe all the time.

Cameron (role of police officer): Parents have control of their kids until they are 18, so parents will do what they have to do to keep them safe.

Jackie (role of adolescent child): We are already safe at home without being monitored by video surveillance. Don't we have some basic human rights?

Garret (role of "Big Data" collector): Why are the kids nervous if they have nothing to hide?

Sammie (role of adolescent child): And why are the parents upset about someone watching *them* when they feel justified in watching *us*?

Connie (role of child): Parents should trust us so that we can learn from our independence.

Sharon (role of parent): We trust our kids, but want to keep them safe.

Sammie (role of adolescent child): What safety issues are in our home? I understand in an amusement park.

Ashton (role of parent): There are other factors, like a fire breaks out.

Connie (role of child): I can understand about parents wanting video surveillance at home. You want to make sure you are safe. You won't be doing anything wrong.

Garret (role of "Big Data" collector): Like I said before, why are the kids nervous if they have nothing to hide?

Ashton (role of parent) (in regard to "Big Data" collecting information): What data would you collect?

Garret (role of "Big Data" collector): The data are searches and purchases. That enables us to target ads that are particular to you. We are not interested in what you are purchasing.

Sharon (role of parent): How do we know if our information is safe?

Garret (role of "Big Data" collector): I am sure that the marketing firms won't do anything else with the data. It is simply to target ads that are more appealing to you.

Sharon (role of parent): I think it is too personal in that sense . . . [inaudible] to extract money from you.

Garret (role of "Big Data" collector): It is just an ad to your interest and you can decide.

Sharon (role of parent): Monitoring your kids is different because you are interested in their safety.

Garret (role of "Big Data" collector): [Collecting data] is mutually beneficial. You can save money in the long run, by offering you deals, selling products, and creating jobs.

Sammie (role of adolescent child): You [parent] see something wrong with people monitoring *you*, but you are watching me heating up some pizza puffs.

Ashton (role of parent): The ads are manipulating you to buy stuff.

Sharon (role of parent): It is creepy that someone knows about what I have purchased and what I am interested in.

Garret (role of "Big Data" collector): Some people do use the ads. Our job is to increase people using the ads.

Connie (role of child): Aren't you just making it easier to find what you want?

Garret (role of "Big Data" collector): The ads are just like when you see a billboard on the highway. If there are ads, you can just ignore them.

Sammie (role of adolescent child): Mom doesn't like the idea that someone is watching you. It is more like technology is watching you.

Mr. Minton: OK, we have covered a lot of issues here today. Some of you were worried about invasions of privacy, including the hacking into systems that were meant to protect you. There are a lot of issues about safety, including worrying about how companies might store, share, or leak information. We'll continue to talk about these problems as we think about how we respond to authority.

A scan of the interchanges in the transcript above reveals students exercising several procedures. These procedures include making claims about the facts of the case and about policy positions. Students offer counterclaims, prompting their peers to support their claims by citing and analyzing evidence, with the evidence typically taking the form of a hypothetical example. In citing examples, students draw from their readings of news stories, which means they are able to summarize. Some claims amount to the assertion of rules; for example, "Parents have control of their kids until they are 18, so parents will do what they have to do to keep them safe." In the face of such an assertion, other students offer competing rules; for example, "We are already safe at home without being monitored by video surveillance. Don't we have some basic human rights?" and "Parents should trust us so that we can learn from our independence."

In the inquiry process, which depends a great deal on students' purposeful interactions, the learners themselves become important sources of information. The students have not all read the same articles, so the process must rely on their contributing what they know from their reading. The teacher might prompt students to elaborate about the reading, if the reference is unclear, or the sharing of information might be a natural element in the conversational exchange. Here is one example: "The data are searches and purchases. That enables us to target ads that are particular to you. We are not interested in what you are purchasing." The learners have to take this new information into account in making their judgments about the appropriateness of the monitoring of the behavior of others. In the end, students consider the facts of the situation (i.e., the Casto family case, the information from their reading, the sharing of information across groups, and the teacher's contributions), recognize the assertion of certain rules or warrants (e.g., "Monitoring your kids is different because you are interested in their safety"; "You [parent] see something wrong with people monitoring *you*, but you are watching me heating up some pizza puffs"; "It is creepy that someone knows about what I have purchased and what I am interested in"), and weigh the value of one rule against another (i.e., the responsibility to monitor and protect against the need for privacy and individual freedom). All of these moves are important for the students' subsequent writing, and the immersion into these procedures through the dialogic exchanges allows students to work with the kind of thinking that writing requires.

ATTENTION TO OTHER LANGUAGE DETAILS

The students' work with a problem-based case exposes them to some vocabulary that is possibly new to them, not as a disconnected list of words, but as concepts that they need to know in order to make sense of the case. Here are some possibilities that a teacher might emphasize and might help the students to understand from the context in which the words are used: *alibi, kiosk, vendors, intrusion, municipalities, sensor, simultaneous, monitor, surveillance, entities,* and *escalate.* I have little confidence that students will understand these words simply by looking up definitions in a dictionary. Instead, I suggest that the teacher find ways to incorporate some of this language as part of daily classroom discourse, and that the teacher also demonstrate ways to infer some meanings from the context of the reading of the case narrative. In addition, students should be familiar with the following academic terms and the procedures that these concepts suggest: *essay, position, justify, summarize, respond, point of view, argue,* and *introduce.* In some ways, these terms express goals, in the sense of what students are expected to be able to do. A teacher will likely want to judge whether students have already been exposed to these terms and the actions they suggest, and might want to take time to model what students will be expected to do when they *summarize an argument* or *justify their position*, or *respond to an opposing argument.*

The inquiry process in this case involves some research outside of the classroom, namely, the reading of brief news articles. If the articles are going to inform the discussion and support the inquiry process, the students will need to be able to summarize what they have read for the sake of their small group in preparation for whole-class discussion. Some students will do this readily, but it probably would not be a wasted effort for the teacher to demonstrate how to summarize an article, especially if it advances an argument relative to the central issues in the case. I can imagine the teacher's modeling of summarization strategies and learners' practice with the strategies prior to the work that requires learners to summarize.

INVITATION TO A WRITTEN RESPONSE

The following prompt invites the students to draw from their readings and discussions and from the teacher's demonstrations to produce a position statement about the issues suggested by the case. The prompt begins another process, one in which the students make their attempts, consult with one another and with the teacher, and work their compositions to greater and greater levels of refinement. While the prompt sets a process in motion, the instructions in the prompt link directly to what students have been doing all along as part of their inquiry: identify a problem, express a position in response to the controversy, support a position, identify and assess competing positions, summarize and reiterate. For the teacher who has designed an inquiry sequence, these instructions link directly to the procedures that students have practiced all along as elements in their discussions.

Prompt for "The Parents Are Watching"

The experience of the Casto family illustrates a conflict that affects individual families and society as a whole. Parents in families and elected officials and civil servants in government recognize a responsibility to protect children and community members from harm. At the same time, the people who might need protection also have an interest in protecting their privacy and in exercising their freedom of movement, liberated from the prying eyes of others. Individuals also might enjoy several conveniences that follow from businesses recognizing their consumer needs and interests. However, many consumers also resent the fact that strangers are tracking their searches and purchases, and perhaps sharing this information with others, in order to profile the consumers in an effort to sell them more goods and services.

Write a *position statement* about the issues described above. In a fully developed essay, address the following questions:

- What is the *central problem* that you have been discussing with your classmates and reading about?
- What is your *position* in regard to the tension between security and privacy, and between convenience and privacy?
- How do you *justify* the position you hold?

- Other reasonable *people are likely to disagree with you*. What position do they embrace? How do they justify their position? Why do you disagree with their justification?
- How would you summarize the problem and your position in response to the problem?

Remember that you are writing for some interested readers who have not been part of our class discussions and have not read what we have read. You will need to provide sufficient detail to help your readers to understand the controversy and your arguments.

SAMPLE RESPONSE

The following representative essay is the product of the inquiry process. The essay reveals in many ways how the writer benefited from the interactions with peers, from her individual research, and from the sharing of distributed knowledge across a class.

SAFETY AND PRIVACY: A BALANCING ACT

FIONA CADOGAN

Safety of the general public is a very important subject; it is a responsibility of each community to make sure that it has this protection. Disagreement, however, comes up when debating how many cautions need to be put in place so people are safe. If an agreement could be made on how many protective devices and safety cautions are needed to keep everyone safe, then everyone would be able to feel more secure in their daily lives. Many measures, such as video cameras, GPS tracers, and corporate business trackers, are taken to ensure the safety of people; but the extent of these cautions should be to provide the best protection possible to each age group, while, at the same time, not invading a person's privacy.

Safety measures should be more directed toward children than adults, but overall, everyone needs to be able to feel secure; these cautions also need to not interfere with one's privacy. Since adults know more than children about dangers in the world, adults have more responsibility, because they would know if what they're doing is wrong. In most cases, children are innocent and want to believe everyone is good, but adults know better and need to make it their job to protect children from harm. They use general security techniques like video cameras, GPS tracers, and corporate business trackers. These devices all help to make sure nothing bad happens, because they can focus on suspicious actions or posts; they also notify authorities to stop situations from happening. In the case "The Parents Are Watching," Mr. and Mrs. Casto track their children from a GPS app on their cell phones. In this way, they are able to know where their children are and if they are supposed to be there. These tools can be overused. For example, video footage could be leaked, GPS tracers can be a key factor in stalking, and a business tracker could be misused by keeping all addresses. The Casto parents installed video cameras all over their house, so the children don't feel comfortable in their own house. This misuses the technology since it's supposed to help a person feel secure, not insecure. Yes, the parents could keep their children safe from all harm, but they ruined their trust with their kids, since they made too much effort to see what they were doing. In the end, it all comes down to the factor of who is using these security measures and why. These tools should only be used by trusted figures, so everyone is protected without having their privacy taken away.

Most of the problems on public safety also develop around the different opinions from different types of people. Parents feel they have every right to control their child's life. Police figure it is OK for them to do a random search on any person to make sure they're not doing anything suspicious. Companies believe they can track their consumers' usage of their products, so they can make their products better. According to the *New York Times*, "Simply asking for name and address information poses many challenges: transcription errors, increased checkout time and, worse yet, losing customers who feel that you're invading their privacy." Like the *Times* suggests, businesses are going to lose customers if they continue stalking their usage of their products. All of these invasions of privacies lead to loss of trust. Security measures need to be taken, but compromises need to be involved for everyone to benefit. Parents have every right to monitor their children, but they should trust them enough to know they won't put themselves in dangerous positions. Police should be allowed to search people, but it should be of someone who is a suspect, not a random person. Companies could send out surveys instead of tracking their customers' usage of their items. If compromises similar to these were made, safety cautions would be met, and people's privacies wouldn't be invaded.

Protective measures are different depending on age, but they should all ensure safety and respect a person's privacy. What could happen without safety cautions in place is a scary thought. This is why the debate in the extent to which safety measures should be taken is such a big deal. All in all, the best method of protection is keeping the general public safe without intruding in one's personal space.

FEATURES OF THE RESPONSE

The length of this response reveals in itself that the writer has invested considerable thought and energy in learning about the issues at the heart of the case and in planning an elaborated analysis. The introduction to the essay illustrates that the writer is familiar enough with the issues related to security and individual rights to frame a problem for the reader to anticipate and think about.

The writer appears to have benefited from her own research and from the research completed by others. She cites a specific passage from a news article to illustrate the benefits and dangers attached to monitoring and surveillance. She does not dismiss one side of the question in favor of the other. In fact, the writer admits the value in some surveillance in public places, but offers guidelines for checking the extent of the surveillance.

I judge that Fiona's essay above is the product of her inquiry, which involved discussions with classmates on at least three levels: small-group work, role-playing to simulate a community meeting, and a whole-class discussion in which students advanced their own arguments. The earlier transcript of the related class discussion, which was part of a series of discussions, reveals that learners use the interactions with peers as opportunities to work out their arguments. They contend with opposing views and exceptions, and offer the rationale for their own positions. Various contributors to the discussion share what they know from their small-group discussions and from their related reading. All of this talk, I suggest, positioned students to write elaborated responses about the contemporary problem of protecting privacy while taking appropriate measures for safety and security.

While the students appear to have benefited from class discussion, each student had to plan individually, share a draft with partners, and work the composition into a more refined state. But much went into the preparation that supported individual planning and contributed to the process of producing an elaborated and refined response to the case and to the broader issues that it suggests. And all along the way, discussion was at the heart of inquiry and composing.

REFLECTING ON PROCEDURES AND APPLYING THEM AGAIN

I recognize a great deal of value in following an inquiry process to help students to produce elaborated, organized, logical, and coherent responses to a complicated issue. I conclude also that the experience of participating in a process of shared inquiry about the case represented above would prepare learners for thinking critically about some imaginative literature that depicts authoritarian societies and warns the reader about dangers associated with the loss of human rights. In the long run, the more important outcome is that the learners move away from the current inquiry experience with a conscious awareness of the procedures that they followed in order to deliberate with others, research a complex problem, and produce a quality written response. The students who participated in the inquiry related to the issues raised by the case "The Parents Are Watching" are likely to be aware that they relied on the following procedures:

- Read and summarized news stories
- Noted their peers' summaries of news stories
- Connected a series of texts in judging how they informed the learner's thinking about a current issue
- Deliberated in discussion by attending to and evaluating their peers' contributions and offering their own insights, judgments, and questions
- Constructed arguments about a significant policy proposition
- Composed an elaborated analysis by framing a problem for an outside reader, synthesizing readings and discussions to reveal critical issues, citing evidence to support claims, invoking general principles to interpret evidence, and evaluating alternative views
- Attributed appropriately the sources of information used to support claims

These procedures align well with the language of the Common Core State Standards and represent important proficiencies for college and career readiness and for responsible citizenship. If students have command of these many procedures, they should be able to put them to work again to support their own inquiry into other critical issues that they find personally compelling. In fact, a teacher might formalize this process of transferring and expanding inquiry by taking the following measures:

- Prompt students to write a reflection about how they were able to produce the written response that they completed, or facilitate a conversation with the whole class about the processes students followed in their research and writing: Now that you have written an elaborated composition about a complex problem, explain to someone else how you were able to do this.
- Schedule a current activity that allows the students to apply the same procedures again, whether this new activity involves an investigation into a related work of imaginative literature, or the students' self-directed inquiry into critical and complex issues that attract their attention.

I would expect that after reflection on the writing they had just completed, students would have a conscious awareness of an inquiry process. I would hope that they wouldn't set these procedures aside, but soon have another opportunity to engage in the process to arrive at deeper understandings about complex texts and critical issues. I also would want students to have the confidence that they could apply and adapt the procedures whenever needed.

The descriptions above emphasize active participation in small- and large-group discussions. But, as Schultz (2009) points out, *participation* does not necessarily mean that students have to be overtly active in contributing to the conversations. Schultz makes a strong case that the less talkative students may be contributing in subtle ways and benefiting from the generally dialogic experience:

> At times, silence is a form of participation. Importantly, we can explore *what* a person contributes to a conversation or a classroom as well as *how* he participates. If the contribution is verbose, yet only tangentially related to the topic, it may be less important than the short statement or gesture that shifts the direction of the discussion and illuminates the learning or a statement that comes after silence and reflection. The notion of building democratic practice hinges on reframing classroom participation as engaged participation whether verbal or silent, through auditory or visual modes. (p. 119, emphasis in the original)

In the discussions that I represent in this book, I emphasize what students *say*. My method has been to collect audio recordings and then transcribe them to analyze what was said. I acknowledge, however, that this method does not account for the less overt signs of engagement, and I judge that many students benefit from small-group and large-group discussions in many forms, whether the students are more active players or silent or subtle reflectors on the experience. A teacher might look for nonverbal clues about students' engagement: their nods of agreement or disagreement; their movement forward to attend to a speaker; their smiles, laughter, or gasps; and their evidence of note-taking. Often written work that follows discussions such as those described above will reveal references to the discussions, suggesting a benefit even to the quietest of classmates.

THE PRODUCT OF INQUIRY PROCEDURES

In the student example above, the form of the composition apparently derives from the writer's understanding of the requirements of the task; that is, the goals that she wants to accomplish, her understanding of the needs and existing knowledge of an audience, her own understanding of the complexities of the policy question, her assessment of the views of others who might disagree with her, and an appreciation of a quality standard for writing, a standard that apparently includes demands for logical and organized thought, coherent construction of content, and precise and "correct" use of language. Instead of relying on a generic form to guide the production of a composition, the writer followed a more complex inquiry path that engaged her in using procedures that are reliable enough and flexible enough to foster strong thinking and mature expression in many situations. If teachers are going to take to heart the goals expressed in the Common Core State Standards and to assess students' proficiencies relative to those standards, they will want to move learners away from templates and formulas and promote more authentic processes that foster careful and critical thinking and mature expression.

In learning important processes for thinking about problems and composing logical and elaborated responses, students benefit from their interactions with peers. We know from the research literature (Graham & Perin, 2007a, 2007b; Hillocks, 1986a; Nystrand,1997) that students who engage in authentic discussions with peers are likely to produce better, more elaborated writing than they would have if they did not have the opportunity to work with peers. There is a clear positive correlation: More opportunities to talk to peers as part of the writing process translate into higher quality, more elaborated compositions. It is worthwhile, then, to look closely at what happens during peer interactions that could account for the benefit that they produce. This is what the following chapters seek to illustrate.

CHAPTER 3

Inquiry: Teachers' Plans and Learners' Outcomes

The purposeful discussions and the elaborated writing that derives in large part from those discussions are products of teachers' careful planning and skillful management. We can see inquiry in action by following the work of two 5th-grade teachers who see inquiry, discussion, and writing as powerful tools to help students learn concepts in their school's social studies curriculum. The curriculum begins with a unit about "First Americans," a study of Native Americans who lived in North America before the incursions of European settlers. The teachers knew from experience with this unit that students approach the reading of the textbook unenthusiastically and are generally bored with the study of people who lived long ago and seem odd and foreign to them. To begin the planning for the unit, the teachers identified a problem that would initiate an inquiry process and was likely to foster student engagement in the study of Native American tribes, especially during early colonial days. They judged that a critical assessment about a proposed bill to provide *reparations* for various Native American "tribes" might give significance and coherence to the social studies unit, and that the students' discussions and related writing might serve the learners in mastering the subject content. The teachers decided that the students' written assessment of a proposed bill would follow a simulated legislative hearing at which students representing various tribes would present testimonies and answer questions posed by "legislators."

PLANNING FOR SIGNIFICANT OUTCOMES

The planning process began with a close examination of what students would be expected to do. Two questions guided the examination: (1) What do students need to know? (2) What do students need to be able to do? The following writing prompt represents the summative assessment for the unit. While the teachers had a clear picture of where they wanted students to end up, they needed to plan the learning experiences that would equip the learners with the content knowledge and procedural knowledge that would be necessary to produce a meaningful written response. The language of the prompt is complicated for 5th-graders, obviously requiring some assistance from the teachers to help the learners understand what they would be expected to do.

THE REQUEST FOR REPARATIONS

Directions: The members of a committee of the Congress of the United States seek your advice about proposed action on a bill to provide *reparations* for Native American tribes. The brief story below describes the problem. You will want to talk about the story with two or three of your classmates before you decide the appropriate action to recommend.

THE STORY

Members of several Native American tribes have petitioned members of the United States House of Representatives to pass a bill (a new law) that would guarantee *reparations for all members of their tribes*. The tribes include Mohawk, Powhatan, Iroquois, and Delaware (Lenape). They understand that the principle behind the idea of *reparations* is that the central government of the United States, representing the whole nation, must take collective responsibility for the many harms experienced by the Native Americans since the arrival of European settlers to the continent. Under this idea of reparations, the government is held responsible for not adequately protecting people from harm, and in some instances for causing or continuing the harm. The advocates for the reparations bill point to the following harms as cause for reparations:

- Deceptive and unfair treaties that took ancestral lands from the tribes and displaced them to live on reservations located on far less desirable lands
- Physical attacks on Native American communities, causing serious injury, torture, deaths, and the destruction of property
- Deceptive trade practices that cheated Native Americans out of valuable artifacts and other property or assets
- Enslavement of members of Native American tribes
- The spread of deadly viral diseases never before known to Native Americans
- The suppression of Native American culture, including language, religion, education, medicine, and the arts, driving these elements to near extinction
- The humiliating depiction of Native Americans as godless, ignorant savages, subject to ridicule through inappropriately using images and symbols as mascots and commercial brands

Some critics have been quick to point out the harms that Native Americans have caused to European settlers and their descendants. In some instances the critics have recommended that the Native American tribes compensate the descendants of European settlers.

The advocates for the reparations bill would like to see a new law that would guarantee certain compensations for the Native American tribes. They have suggested the following possibilities:

- A *universal apology* that candidly admits the federal government over several generations has sponsored or tolerated the harms to Native Americans

- Monetary compensation for *each* tribe member of at least $10,000

- The return of all tribal lands to the current tribal councils to decide their distribution and future use, even if this means the displacement of current residents on those lands

- The banning of all Native American images and symbols for use as commercial logos and team mascots (e.g., Braves, Indians, Chiefs, Seminoles, Chippewas, etc.)

- A comprehensive program of education in the public schools to inform students about the harms and injustices that European settlers have caused to Native Americans for hundreds of years

- A program of public service messages to elevate the image and prestige of Native American cultures

Talking to Your Partners

Talk to your classmates about these possibilities. *What do you think would be the best way for the federal government to respond to the requests for reparations?* For each action, explain why you think this is fair or unfair compensation for the things that Native Americans claim that they have suffered for hundreds of years. Your judgments should rely on your guidelines for deciding reparations claims. You will want to take notes during the discussion so that you have notes ready for a written response.

Writing to the Chairman of the Committee

Representative Philip Uster wants to know what you think legislators *should do*, if anything, to compensate Native American tribes and to make amends for harms to a whole group of people. *Write a letter to Representative Philip Uster to explain.* Your letter should include the following:

- Since Representative Uster doesn't know why you are writing the letter, begin by *describing briefly* the situation you are writing about.

- *Recommend the actions* that the Congress and the nation should take to repair the damage caused to Native Americans (or to European settlers, if you prefer). For each action that you recommend, *explain why* you think it is necessary and fair. Draw from your research, and the research of classmates, about Native Americans and early settlers, and rely on your guidelines for reparations to make your case.

- If you disagree with any of the demands that Native American tribes have made, explain why these steps would not be appropriate or fair. Again, draw from your research and the research of your classmates, and rely on the guidelines for reparations.

- At the end, *summarize* what you think of the requests for reparations, and what you think the members of Congress should do.

Remember that Representative Philip Uster is a respected authority in the Congress. Your letter should be very carefully written and very neatly presented. As always with writing that you care about, it is a good idea to share your letter with other readers. Sometimes other readers can help you to discover what you left out, where you said too much, where you could be clearer, and where you need to correct some things. Be sure to use your readers' comments to guide you in making any changes before you submit your work.

TASK ANALYSIS AND KNOWLEDGE DOMAINS

A task analysis reveals the many demands that the final writing prompt makes on the 5th-graders. First, the students would have to know a good deal about the Native American tribes identified in the writing prompt. Students would need insight into the cultures of these tribes: where they lived, how they lived, what they valued. Of particular importance, the students would need to know about the specific events that occurred when Native Americans encountered the settlers from Europe, whether those encounters ended in atrocities against the native tribes or abuses against the settlers. Perhaps some encounters were copacetic, at least initially. If we drill deeper into the prompt, we realize that the students would have to read on their own, take notes, share information with teammates, and select what was important for testifying in the simulated legislative hearing.

Much of the research that students completed would equip them with the declarative knowledge that would be useful in making judgments and supporting claims. Teachers had to model both print and digital means for gathering information about the culture clashes between Native Americans and European settlers, and the students needed time to collect and synthesize the information that they gathered. The teachers recognized that some students would need help in understanding the vocabulary of the writing prompt, so the teachers found opportunities to weave the key vocabulary into the lessons that preceded the research and exposure to the final writing task.

But the teachers recognized that the students also needed to develop the procedures that would be important for evaluating events and judging them against a standard for deciding whether reparations were necessary and, if so, what the reparations should be. In advancing an argument about a policy question about proposed reparations, the students would need to have a firm sense of the criteria against which they could judge the necessity for reparations and the form of the reparations. In other words, they had to establish some rules or standards for making critical judgments. In the end, all the information that the students gathered through their research would have limited value unless they were aware of some reasonable guidelines for judging whether the events described in their reports demonstrated cause for reparations and for establishing what responses count as appropriate repairs.

Consistent with the principles for curriculum design sponsored by Wiggins and McTighe (2005), and the more detailed guidelines for building units of instruction for English language arts described by Smagorinsky (2007), the 5th-grade teachers planned backwards from their expressed goals for learning. A key step in the sequence was to prepare students to express their own guidelines for knowing when reparations were appropriate and for deciding what repairs were appropriate. The teachers understood from experience with young learners that they already knew a thing or two about expectations for repairing damage done by another. They might already have in mind the conditions under which they would forgive another, or the steps necessary to rectify an unfair act by a parent or sibling. These everyday situations were closer to the 5th-graders' experiences than the problems associated with the incursions of White Europeans into North America, although the principles involved with repairing the harms that one causes another remain the same. The teachers judged that their students already knew a good deal about the concept of *reparations*, but the learners needed to tackle some specific everyday problems in order to become aware of the principles that guided their decisions, and to express these principles as warrants that would become important for their oral testimonies and written responses.

In a sense, then, the process of preparing to write a critical assessment of a legislator's proposed bill begins with a teacher introducing the students to a set of problem-based scenarios. Since the 5th-graders have seldom or never had opportunities to discuss scenarios in their small groups, the teacher models the process by facilitating discussion of the first scenario for the whole class. The teacher begins by reading the first scenario aloud:

> During a dispute about the use of a friend's jump rope, 8-year-old
> Stella Jenkins bit her neighbor, 7-year-old Lucy Madison. The bite on
> Lucy's forearm hurt very much, drew a little blood, and left Lucy in
> tears. After Lucy reported the incident to her mother, Mrs. Madison
> brought Lucy back to the Jenkins home, described the scene to Mrs.
> Jenkins, and demanded an apology from Stella to Lucy. Reluctantly,

Stella said, "OK. I'm sorry. So there." Lucy was not satisfied. Her arm still hurt, and it probably would be bruised for days. Sufficiently traumatized by the attack, Lucy would remain afraid to play with Stella again.

The teacher then asks, "To what extent is the apology a satisfactory repair? If more reparations are necessary, what would you expect? If Stella has done all she could do, how would you explain this to Lucy?" The following exchange is a composite of several discussions across several 5th-grade classes and reveals the function of the modeling and the interactions among the students.

Missy: The way she says it, "So there," doesn't sound like she is really sorry. I don't think that Stella is really sorry, and Lucy won't be happy.
Ginger: Yeah, but how do you make her be sorry?
Bobby: You can't make her be sorry, but she should at least sound like she means it.
Teacher: OK, so you want at least for her to offer a *sincere apology*, even if she might in her heart not really be sincere.
Bobby: Yeah, she has to give a sincere apology.
Suzy: But I don't think that's enough. She *bit* her and hurt her. Doesn't it say that she is still bruised and sore? Stella has to do something nice to make up for hurting her.
Teacher: So you want Stella to do something more. What would that be?
Flavio: I know, I know. She could give her some money.
Ginger: No. I don't know. She could like bake her some cookies.
Bobby: Yeah, that would be good. She's got to apologize and bake some cookies—chocolate chip cookies, no nuts.
Teacher: How does that sound, everyone?
Students: Yeah!
Teacher: So, hold on. Let me see if I can say this so that it sounds like rules that we can use later on. (Writing at a document reader and reciting aloud): First, if someone hurts someone else, he or she (the offender) has to offer a sincere apology. Is that what we are saying?
Duffy: Yeah, but you can't make someone be sincere.
Teacher: I agree, but this rule (pointing to the projected statement) is what we expect. OK, let's try another rule. Let me think. I believe I heard a second rule. Oh, yeah, it goes something like this: If someone hurts someone, the offender needs to do something nice for the hurt person to make up (compensate) for the hurt. Are you saying that's our rule?
Ginger: That's a good rule. I want some cookies now. You made me hungry.

This bit of discussion reveals the teacher's "dialogic bid," as Nystrand (1997) would call it, because the teacher's posing of a specific problem and the related questions suggests that there is an area of actual doubt, about which even the teacher is uncertain. Everyone feels at liberty and equally knowledgeable to offer judgments. The interchanges among the students serve several important functions. Even though the class is exploring an area of doubt, the students all feel confident that each one is as expert as anyone else in the class in making judgments about what the characters depicted in the scenario should do.

The students' reactions to the situation described in the scenario tapped into the values that they hold and that they think should guide decent behavior. As a student expressed something that sounded like a rule, another student or the teacher offered an exception (e.g., "Yeah, but how do you make her be sorry?") or asked for clarification or refinement (e.g., "OK, so you want her at least to offer a *sincere apology*, even if she might in her heart not really be sincere."). As the discussion progressed, and the teacher saw that there appeared to be agreement across the class, the teacher paraphrased the rule and recorded it for everyone to note. The conversation continued to be exploratory, with students trying out their ideas about repair and compensation. When the teacher judged that there had been sufficient discussion about the first scenario, she summarized the agreements and wrote down the statements that would become principles for evaluating a more complicated case. Some research (Smagorinsky & Fly, 1993, 1994) suggests that through the teacher's modeling, the students see the dialogic moves that they can imitate in their own small-group discussions: inviting comments from everyone in the group, testing out any stated rules to see whether they can apply with consistency, paraphrasing often, and summarizing the agreements. Some of these moves are basic to argument: The students agree on the claim that Stella has responsibility for some repair; the scenario itself serves as the example to illustrate the claim; and the expressed rules applied to the example serve as the warrants needed to interpret the story and arrive at the claim.

As the inquiry progressed, the students worked in groups to discuss progressively more complex situations. The teacher recognized that the students could not sustain the small-group discussions for large chunks of time, so she assigned three scenarios at a time and then moved the students back to the large-group forum. The large-group discussion invited greater diversity of thought and allowed individual students reporting for their group to express the whole argument, not just their claims. Working together, a team of teachers designed the following set of scenarios to be progressively more complicated, putting students in a position to judge more ambiguous and perplexing situations (McCann et al., 2012).

What Are Appropriate Reparations?

2. Last summer, Garrick saw his neighbor Benjamin's bicycle lying unattended on the lawn in front of Benjamin's house. Garrick was in a hurry to make it to swim team practice at a pool a mile away, so he took Benjamin's bike and rode it to the pool, with the intention of returning it to Benjamin after practice. But Garrick kept the bike for another 2 weeks, riding to practice, visiting friends, and generally cruising around town. When Benjamin's parents discovered that Garrick had the bike, they demanded that he return it. When Garrick brought the bike back, Benjamin noticed that two spokes were broken, the front wheel rim was bent, and the brakes didn't work properly. Garrick told Benjamin he was sorry, but Benjamin wasn't satisfied. He wanted more. After all, his bike was not in the same condition as it was when it was taken. He was denied use of the bike for 2 weeks when he could have used it to ride to soccer practice and to visit his friends. What, if anything, do you think Garrick owes Benjamin? What would be the appropriate repair for his loss?

3. When Mrs. Stahlwerk visited her sister-in-law Mrs. Ganesdale, Mrs. Stahlwerk accidently knocked a vase off a table and it smashed into several pieces on the floor. Mrs. Ganesdale was appalled, especially because the vase had been a gift from her husband. He purchased it while he was traveling in Japan, and it is unlikely that Mrs. Ganesdale will ever be able to find a replacement. Mrs. Stahlwerk offered to pick up all of the pieces and glue them together as best she could. "It will be as good as new," she said. Mrs. Ganesdale was skeptical. As an alternative, Mrs. Stahlwerk offered to give Mrs. Ganesdale some money, but Mrs. Ganesdale claimed that it was impossible to name a price for such a rare item. "What can I do to make it up to you?" Mrs. Stahlwerk asked. What should Mrs. Stahlwerk do to make up for the damage she caused?

4. In 1908, an experienced burglar named Bud Parnell broke into the home of Alice and Walter Crestfalt and stole their life savings, an amount of $5,000, which they had hidden in their mattress. Parnell invested the stolen money wisely, enabling him to assume a position of prominence in town. When he married and started a family, he was able to send his children to the best schools, including elite private colleges. Equipped with fine educations, the children of Bud Parnell were able to assume leadership positions in their father's many businesses, including real estate ventures and banks. On the other hand, the poor children of Alice and Walter Crestfalt lived in poverty and received very poor educations, which kept them from advancing economically and socially. After Bud Parnell's death, his published memoir revealed that the money that he had stolen financed the advancement of his family, and the loss of the money kept the Crestfalt family in poverty. Now the grandchildren of Walter and Alice demand compensation from the Parnell family. They want much more than the original $5,000. Parnell's grandchildren resist paying anything because they were not personally responsible for the crime. What, if anything,

would be the appropriate compensation that the Parnell family should offer to members of the Crestfalt family? Why do you think your proposal would be fair?

5. About 100 years ago, a city inspector named Basil Pestoli told a couple named Carl and Lillian Rathe that their modest home was situated on a site that emitted deadly radon gas. He told them that they would have to vacate the property, which had become worthless because no one else could occupy it. He offered them no compensation for their home. Carl and Lillian didn't believe Mr. Pestoli at first and they protested to other officials in city government. But the others supported Mr. Pestoli's story. Discouraged, Carl and Lillian packed up all of their belongings and moved far away, receiving nothing for their home. Mr. Pestoli then sold the property to another couple and shared the profits with the others who had shared in his deception. Recently the grandchildren of Carl and Lillian discovered that Mr. Pestoli, who has long been dead, stole their grandparents' property. They now want it back and have demanded that the current occupants move out. Should the current occupants move out without any compensation? If the descendants of Carl and Lillian cannot assume ownership of the house, how else can they be compensated fairly?

6. When Enrico Octavo entered Roosevelt School as a 1st-grader, his teacher, Miss Willingham, told him that he was to be known as Henry (the English equivalent of Enrico) from that day forward. Although Henry's parents were proud immigrants from Italy, Miss Willingham insisted that he never speak Italian in school. "You're American now, and you must speak English like everyone else in Roosevelt School." As the students began to work on their penmanship, Miss Willingham noticed that Henry held his pencil in his left hand. She insisted that he write with his right hand. "Using the left hand is a sign of the devil," said the superstitious Miss Willingham, and she corrected Henry every time he attempted to write with his left hand. By the time Henry reached college, he spoke little Italian, and he wrote right-handed. As he began to reflect more and more on who he was as a person, he decided that Miss Willingham had robbed him of a lot by trying to separate him from his Italian heritage and by forcing him to write right-handed, when using his left hand was more natural. He thought that he would return to Roosevelt School to visit Miss Willingham, if she was still there, and demand some compensation for what she had taken from him. What could Miss Willingham do at this point as reparation for the loss that Henry felt? Why would this be appropriate?

As the students discussed the scenarios in their small groups and with the class as a whole, they found it increasingly difficult to specify a repair or compensation when the victim's loss included abstract values like self-esteem and sense of identity. Many students were uncertain whether or not descendants were to be held responsible for the reprehensible behavior of their ancestors. Their exploratory interactions included expressions of frustration at not being able to decide. But the 5th-graders made their attempts, met challenges, agreed to refinements, and framed their own rules, which they all recorded under the understanding that they needed to be aware of the rules in order to apply them to a more detailed case. Here are the rules concluded by two 5th-grade classes:

- A person should make a sincere apology to a person that he or she hurt.
- If you hurt someone, you should try to do something nice to make up for the injury.
- If you punish someone for hurting others, the punishment should teach a lesson and not just hurt back.
- When it is impossible to put a price on something that was taken or destroyed, you should still make an effort to pay a person back.
- Sometimes a person has to pay back for things his or her parents or grandparents did to harm others.
- Even when someone takes something that can't be returned, he or she has to pay back in some way, like through service projects or other acts of kindness.

As the dialogue above illustrates, the rules, which later serve as warrants, develop from the exploratory talk, with the teacher helping the students to find the language to represent consensus among the many thinkers. As you will see in the next phase of the inquiry process, the learners drew on these rules in order to judge the behavior of some middle school students and to recommend a course of action regarding that behavior.

AN INQUIRY INTO REPARATIONS IN MIDDLE SCHOOL

The classes of 5th-graders that I observed were headed to the neighboring middle school for the next school year. Their teachers knew that among other worries, the students contemplated how older, more aggressive students might treat them with disrespect and perhaps abuse them; so the following case, which precedes the simulated legislative hearing, resonates with them. The focus for the inquiry is not an abstract "essential question," but a contextualized problem that represents potential harms that adolescents actually worry about. The description for the case below parallels the writing prompt that the students see at the end of their legislative hearing. In a sense, students will complete the same task twice: first, write an argument about a policy issue concerning conduct in school; then, write an argument about a broader policy issue concerning the historical mistreatment of whole societies. The procedures that students apply in writing about the more familiar case equip them to apply the same procedures in a more complicated case that relies on the same warrants but draws on a more extensive body of information.

The View from 5th Grade

Directions: The principal, teachers, and students at Joseph Hill Middle School ask for your help in taking the right action toward a current student and a former student at their school. The brief story below describes the source of the problem. You will want to talk about the story with two or three of your classmates before you decide the appropriate action.

The Story

Jimmy Farfel is beginning 8th grade at Joseph Hill Middle School. Since Jimmy was in 3rd grade at John L. Lewis Elementary School, he has been the victim of bullying at the hands of Landon Kramden and his sister Leila. Landon is also entering 8th grade at Joseph Hill Middle School, but his sister Leila graduated in June and is entering 9th grade at Floodrock High School.

Many people at Joseph Hill Middle School have become more sensitive to problems with bullies. They recognize that bullying can take many forms, including physical harm, threats, teasing, and cruel remarks. Bullying has even found its way onto the Internet, where bullies have posted unflattering pictures and mean gossip about fellow students. Part of the problem is that the victims of bullying have been too afraid to tell anyone about the hurt they have suffered. But a recent campaign has encouraged students to come forth with their stories. This has prompted Jimmy Farfel to tell his story about Landon and Leila Kramden. Jimmy claims that the brother and sister have done these things to him:

- Stole lunch money from him, leaving him on many days with nothing to eat for lunch
- Hit him and twisted his arm in a painful position when he resisted giving up his lunch money
- Knocked books out of his hands in crowded hallways and laughed at him as he struggled to pick up scattered papers amid a wave of feet
- Took his graphing calculator for their own use, causing Jimmy to get into trouble with his math teacher for forgetting to bring the calculator to class
- Called him many insulting names in front of other students
- Teased him about wearing a Cubs jersey, because they were Cardinals fans and hated the Cubs
- Threatened to beat him up if he wore any Cubs clothing to school, scaring Jimmy into never wearing the emblem of his favorite team again

- Took a picture of Jimmy when it looked like he was picking his nose on the playground and posted the picture on a website that invited viewers to write cruel comments
- Wrote nasty rumors about Jimmy on the website, including the claim that he had a crush on Mrs. Zeeler, the ancient library assistant at the school

When Dr. Philoman, the principal, talked to Landon about these reports, at first he denied he did any of the things that Jimmy claimed. When other students confirmed that the reports were true, Landon said, "So what? He deserved it. He is such a little twerp." Leila also admitted her role in the bullying, but she said, "I don't even go to that school anymore, so what do you think you can do to me? And a lot of that stuff happened away from school. You have no control over what I do away from school."

Jimmy's parents are quite upset, and they want Landon and Leila to do something to make up for all of the harm that they did to Jimmy. They want both *restitution* (giving money back) and some form of *punitive* action (punishment). They have suggested the following possibilities:

- Giving back all of Jimmy's stolen lunch money, plus a little extra
- Buying Jimmy a new graphing calculator
- Removing all of the harmful and insulting material from the website
- Apologizing to Jimmy in front of his classmates
- Apologizing to the current and former students of Joseph Hill Middle School who might have witnessed the abuse to Jimmy
- Wearing Cubs apparel to school for several days
- Buying Jimmy a new Cubs jersey
- Completing 100 hours of community service each by making anti-bullying posters and by talking to church youth groups about the harms of bullying

TALKING TO YOUR PARTNERS

Talk to your classmates about these possibilities. *What do you think would be the best way for Landon and Leila to make up for the harm they have done to Jimmy?* Do you think any of the actions listed above would be fair? Do you think any of the actions would not be appropriate? Can you think of other actions that have not been listed? For each action, explain why you think this is a fair or unfair compensation for the things that Landon and Leila have done to Jimmy. You will want to take notes during the discussion so that you have notes ready for a written response.

WRITING TO THE PRINCIPAL

Dr. Philoman, principal of Joseph Hill Middle School, wants to know what you think he *should* do, and what he *can* do to force Landon and Leila to make up for what they have done to Jimmy. *Write a letter to Dr. Philoman to explain.* Your letter should include the following:

- Since Dr. Philoman doesn't know why you are writing the letter, begin by *describing briefly* the situation you are writing about. Don't bother introducing yourself. Tell him whether or not Landon and Leila should do something as an attempt to repair or perhaps compensate for the damage that they have done to Jimmy.

- *Recommend the steps* that Landon and Leila should take to make up for the things they have done to Jimmy. For each action, *explain why* you think it is necessary and fair.

- If you disagree with any of the demands that Jimmy's parents have made, explain why these steps would not be appropriate or fair.

- At the end, *summarize* what you think of Landon and Leila's behavior and what you think they should do.

Remember that Dr. Philoman is a respected authority in the school. Your letter should be very carefully written and very neatly presented. As always with writing that you care about, it is a good idea to share your letter with other readers. Sometimes other readers can help you to discover what you left out, where you said too much, where you could be clearer, and where you need to correct some things. Be sure to use your readers' comments to guide you in making any changes before you submit your work.

DISCUSSING THE CASE

As the directions for the case suggest, the students formed teams and began talking about their assessments of the behavior of Leila and Landon, and proposed steps for repair or compensation. The following exchange is a composite of many discussions and represents how students deliberated about the problem:

Sara: These kids are so mean. What is wrong with them?
Billy: The principal has to do something. You got to punish these kids so they stop.
Bradley: That's funny. They put a picture of him picking his nose.
Sara: That's *not* funny. It *looked* like he was picking his nose. That's mean. Someone could take a picture of you doing anything and then put it on the Internet.
Lucy: The sister—what's her name . . . Leila—she doesn't go to the school any more. Can they do anything to her?
Billy: Maybe her parents can do something.

Bradley: They wouldn't let him wear his Cubs stuff. That's funny. The Cubs are stupid anyway.

Lucy: You can't pressure someone to stop wearing their team stuff because you don't like them. You can wear whatever you want.

Teacher (to the whole class): Remember to go back to the rules and see how they apply in this case. Does Jimmy deserve any reparations, any compensation, for what Leila and Landon did to him?

Sara: OK. Then they at least have to say they are sorry.

Billy: And mean it.

Sara: Be sincere about it.

Bradley: How can they make the sister apologize? She doesn't even go to the school.

Sara: We're just saying what she *should* do.

Billy: Maybe they could wear Cubs shirts for a week or something.

Lucy: They would hate that, but I don't see that it will teach them a lesson. They would just get madder, and maybe they would take it out on Jimmy later. They are going to see him in middle school.

Billy: What were our other rules?

Sara: They hurt Jimmy, so they should do something nice for him.

Lucy: I don't think that you can get them to bake cookies or something for Jimmy. But they could do something like community service, like it says. They could talk to other kids about not being bullies.

Bradley: How are you going to get them to do that? Leila doesn't even care. She hates Jimmy.

Billy: They should at least pay him back for the money they took and for his calculator.

Bradley: They don't even know how much they took.

Sara: They know what a calculator costs, and they could guess the rest. The principal could charge the parents. You got to get the parents to do something about this.

The small-group discussions continued along these lines, with students largely exploring their positions about what to do with Leila and Landon. They grappled with the question of what actions to take, judging what would be an appropriate punishment for the offenses. The teacher urged them to refer to their established rules, which became the warrants for interpreting Leila's and Landon's actions. In a sense, they tested their recommendations against the gravity of the students' behavior and against the warrants that define appropriate actions for reparations.

Bradley is the one dissenting voice in the small-group exchange. He appears to be the cynical voice, reminding everyone about the limited hope that the principal can force any repair on any student outside of his supervision in his own school. But Bradley's expressed skepticism is an important element in the conversation, an element that the teachers do not want to suppress. In the face of Bradley's skepticism, the other discussants have to provide support for their positions or otherwise account for the probability that the principal cannot enforce the proposed repairs on at least one of the bullies.

FROM TALKING TO WRITING

After allowing sufficient time for the students to discuss the case in small groups, the teacher in each classroom brought the whole class together to offer their conclusions and analyses. As one would imagine, while the small-group talk is more exploratory in nature, the contributions during the large-group discussion are more fully developed arguments, based on the arguments that the students constructed in probing fashion in their groups. An observer can see an immediate contrast between the small-group work and the large-group discussion: The contributions in the large-group forum are longer and more tightly constructed; the speakers in the large group emphasize the warrants that they have used to interpret events; and the challenges among the whole class focus mostly on the warrants—both their viability as rules and their applicability in the case.

The series of activities, including the discussions about the scenarios and the discussions about the case, help to prepare the learners to write elaborated arguments. But the teachers did not simply engage the learners in discussions and then direct them to write. The process involved a good deal of follow-through, including review of the requirements listed in the prompt, the modeling of various planning processes, drafting, conferencing with the teacher and with peers, and then revising and editing, some of which was never completed to the students' satisfaction.

I will say more about the extended writing process in the next chapter. For now, I offer a portion of one student's writing to link the composition to the discussions that preceded it (see also McCann et al., 2012).

Excerpt from a Case Analysis

Erin Anderson

To me, these cruel acts are unfair and unacceptable. It is time to work with the parents to find appropriate punishments. Landon and Leila have admitted what they have done, but they don't see the harm. So I think we should choose a punishment that opens their eyes. Some punishments that the parents might agree to would have Leila and Landon buying Jimmy a new calculator and doing 100 hours of community service. I think this is fair because it shows them what they did was wrong. After this punishment they shouldn't ever think of bullying anyone ever again. When they learn what they did was wrong, it will bring out the best in them.

I didn't choose the other possible punishments because they're unfair to the bullies. For example, if I chose the punishment of wearing Cubs jerseys to school, that doesn't change who they are and teach them what they did was wrong. I didn't pick these other options because they don't teach.

It appears from this excerpt that Erin paid attention to claims about the possibility that the principal could not enforce punishment with at least one of the bullies. She offers instead that the principal work with the parents to advance two repairs: compensation for the loss of property and service to the community to balance the harm done to the community. She apparently also drew from discussions to note that while the wearing of the jerseys of a hated team might be hurtful to Leila and Landon, this distasteful action would punish them but not necessarily instruct them. Erin draws from the warrants developed in earlier discussions to apply them to the current case to formulate her advice for the principal's policy.

FURTHER COMPLICATIONS

The past is prologue. The series of discussions and exploratory writing prepared students for the more significant inquiry into how to judge the need for and the form of reparations when it appears that one society has perpetrated harms against another society. Equipped with the warrants necessary for interpreting data, and having practiced with the procedures for argument, the students moved forward with the study of Native American tribes in the inquiry-based context of evaluating the merits of proposed legislation that would guide reparations for certain tribes. The following instructions initiated the inquiry from research to discussion-based exploration to written response.

LEGISLATIVE HEARING—
INQUIRY INTO POSSIBLE REPARATIONS
FOR NATIVE AMERICAN TRIBES

Background: Members of the legislature have been considering requests to write a bill to provide reparations for several Native American tribes. If passed, the bill would become a law requiring the government to make amends for past harms to the Native American tribes. The tribes claim that they have been harmed financially, physically, culturally, and socially. Not everyone likes the idea of the bill. Some people point to the harms that the Native Americans inflicted on settlers from Europe and deny that the tribes deserve any reparations.

It is common for a committee of the legislature to conduct a hearing to collect information before anyone attempts to write a bill. The purpose of the current hearing is to find answers to the following questions:

- Has anyone been hurt?
- If someone has been hurt, how significant or bad was the injury?
- Has anything already been done to correct the injury and to make sure that it doesn't occur again?
- What should be done to repair the injury? Why should this action be taken? (How do these actions meet the "rules" for reparations?)
- How will the new actions help?

Preparation: Before legislators can hold a hearing, they have to find people who are knowledgeable about the subject of their hearing. In this case, they have to rely on people who know about the history of the tribes and the history of the settlers who came into contact with the tribes. In other words, the committee members want to hear from a group of experts.

In order to gather the information that will be the focus for the hearing, teams of investigators need to research the following groups:

- Powhatan
- Mohawk
- Delaware (Lenni Lenape)
- Seneca
- Early settlers (New England, New York, and Pennsylvania)

Research assistants and the legislative librarian will help each team to find information about the tribes and the early settlers. Each team will gather information in order to *write a report* to *present at a hearing* and will need to *be prepared to answer questions* from the legislators on the committee.

Here is what your team will need to find out:

1. *Life of the tribe or settlement:* Where and how did the tribe or the settlers live? What were the language and the key elements in the culture of the tribe or settlement? What made the group distinctive?

2. *First encounters:* What were the first encounters between Native Americans and settlers like? To what extent did they initially live peacefully and in support of each other?

3. *Evidence of abuse:* What evidence do you have that settlers caused harm to the tribe, or that tribes caused harm to the settlers? To what extent were people hurt

physically? To what extent were people hurt financially, including the loss of land? To what extent did people lose some elements of the way they liked to live (e.g., language, customs, ties to a particular place, etc.)?

4. *Calculation of repairs:* Considering the established guidelines for reparations, what, if anything, do you recommend as reparation for a particular group?

5. *Answers to questions:* What questions do you think that the legislative committee might have for you? How can you answer the questions that you expect to be asked?

You might want different members of your team to collect information on different questions so that each person is an expert on at least one topic. After collecting the necessary information, your team will need to produce a *written report*. You can look at the *sample report* to give you an idea of what your report should look like. When the committee hearing begins, someone from your team will read the report out loud. Everyone on your team should be prepared to answer questions.

Procedures for Hearing: One person from each team will serve on the legislative committee. There also will be a committee chair who will set the agenda and direct the actions of the committee. Here is the general agenda:

1. Opening of meeting and expression of goal

2. Testimony (reading written statement) and questions and answers

3. Reactions from committee members

4. Vote to recommend reparations after all team representatives have testified

Written Report: After the hearing, all the committee members will return to their original teams. Each team will revise and refine the team's written report. The various reports during the hearing and the answers to questions are likely to provide more information to include in your complete report.

The steps in researching the tribes and settlers, the reports and argument moves in deliberations during the simulated hearing, and the subsequent discussions about the harms and possible responses all contributed to the students' preparation for writing elaborated responses. The collision of opposing ideas about whether reparations were necessary and the form they might take gave significance to the study of the "First Americans" and provided focus and direction for research, discussion, and writing. Again, the teachers and the learners had to follow through with the composing process; but each learner approached the writing with substantial content knowledge, derived in part from tapping into the knowledge distributed across a class of researchers, and with an understanding of the procedures necessary to appeal logically to an audience that was in a position to take action about a policy question.

GOALS AND TEACHERS' THINKING

This chapter shows two 5th-grade teachers at work. In planning instruction, they judged that students' active involvement in a simulated legislative hearing focused on the issue of proposed reparations for Native Americans would lead to several significant learning outcomes. First, they expected that their students would learn substantial social studies content, so that at the end of the unit each student could answer these questions:

- Who were the Native American tribes/nations who lived in the Northeast and in the areas that came to be known as the Mid-Atlantic states in the United States?
- How did these tribes live? What were defining elements in their cultures?
- What were the initial and long-term experiences of the tribes in their encounters with European settlers to the region?
- What were the experiences of European settlers as they founded communities in the lands that were once common to Native Americans?

In preparation for the hearing, the students learned and applied procedures for research, including these specific skills: finding sources of information, judging the relevance and accuracy of sources of information, judging the reliability of sources of information, selecting and synthesizing various sources of information relevant to a research focus, and organizing research notes to support subsequent products and performances.

The inquiry into the reparations issue involved students reading both fiction and nonfiction texts related to Native Americans and their encounters with European settlers. The students responded to their reading through discussion and through written summaries and analyses. The students linked various readings to one another. While researching the central problem, the learners expanded their reading and writing vocabulary. They advanced their reading fluency through the volume and variety of texts they read.

In preparation for the legislative hearing and in response to the hearing, the 5th-graders wrote elaborated arguments to address a significant policy question. In these written arguments, students represented fairly and accurately the opposing views and evaluated the merits of these competing positions. Drawing from their research, the students presented information and analysis in oral reports. As a group, the 5th-graders deliberated about a significant policy question and worked toward consensus. They worked collaboratively with members of a research team, which sometimes required appropriate conflict-resolution strategies, such as paraphrasing to clarify understanding, withholding judgments, and finding common understanding.

In planning instruction, the teachers had to think carefully about the goals for learning so that they knew in substantial detail what demands these target outcomes made on the learners. Essentially, they completed a task analysis. They did not complete this task analysis in a vacuum, but considered who the learners were, judging from their experience with the current group, and reflecting on previous experience, to determine what the 5th-graders already knew. This task analysis guided the planning of specific learning activities. As the chapter illustrates, the teachers planned backwards from the target outcomes, envisioning a sequence in which students would, at each stage, develop the content knowledge and procedures that they would need to proceed to the next step. The preparations at various stages—research, presentations, reading, and writing—involved discussions, and these discussions linked together, with each one building on the previous ones. As the students progressed, the teachers monitored the discussions to look for evidence that students were engaged in the procedures that would be important for writing arguments about the cases. As a whole, the unit of instruction integrated speaking, listening, reading, research, and writing. The teachers did not proceed by targeting isolated skills for students to learn and practice without an overarching purpose. In other words, the teachers did not work their way through a list of learning standards without providing students with a compelling reason to apply the procedures suggested by the standards. Instead, the teachers engaged the learners in thinking about a significant policy problem and in applying various skills and processes in a holistic effort to understand and apply procedures for tangible purposes. The learners relied on inquiry-driven discussions and writing as vehicles for learning social studies content. They also learned important protocols for deliberating civilly and rationally in small-group and large-group forums, even when issues could be hotly contested.

CHAPTER 4

A Structured Process for Inquiry and Writing

In the previous chapters, I have argued that through the several authentic discussions in which learners engage before they write, the students learn important procedures for thinking and composing, and they produce higher quality and more elaborated compositions than they would have if they had not had the opportunity to interact with peers. But I acknowledge that students do not simply talk a lot to their peers in class and then automatically and inevitably produce clear, coherent, refined, and elaborated compositions. The small-group and large-group discussions are part of a wider sequence or "structured process" (Applebee, 1986; Smagorinsky et al., 2010) that relies heavily on frontloaded preparation but follows through with planning, drafting, and refining. This chapter follows the work of teachers and learners to illustrate how the talk transfers and transforms into writing.

BUILDING SCAFFOLDS FOR INQUIRY, DISCUSSION, AND WRITING

If we take, for example, the 5th-grade teachers whose work I describe in Chapter 3, we can get a sense of the broader process involved in learning to write mature academic essays. The process begins before the learners tackle the inquiry-based problem about *reparations*. The teachers noted two preliminary and necessary considerations: (1) If students are going to write logical arguments in support of a proposition about a policy question (i.e., reparations or no reparations), they need to know how to formulate and express arguments; and (2) if students are going to produce high-quality work and support one another in the effort to refine their writing, they need to have in mind a quality standard for writing in general and for writing arguments for specific audiences.

One 5th-grade teacher, Ms. Boski, offered this insight: "We wanted kids to write arguments, but we worried that they would think about arguments in the negative way that people commonly talk about argument—like, 'That couple got into a bad argument,' or 'Don't *argue* with me.' We want kids to understand that when we talk about *argument*, we are simply talking about logical thinking. So before we get to the more complicated problem, with the research and the reporting and discussions, we wanted our students to practice with a simpler problem and see that there is a standard for determining if someone's expressed thoughts were logical." This is a common recognition of the importance of scaffolding, in the sense that the teacher will build on the knowledge that the learners already have, and will continue to build from the simple to the complex.

In this instance, early in the school year, the teachers introduced their students to an easily recognizable problem. The teachers described a local family that had difficulty in agreeing on a destination for the family vacation. The inquiry-based activity introduced students to basic components of argument, and revealed argument as a tool for solving problems, especially when the solution called for negotiation and compromise. The teachers surmised that the students' work in small groups and as a whole class would involve them in summarizing, representing fairly and accurately the competing views, advancing their own arguments civilly and rationally, and reflecting on the process of problem solving. A description of the activity follows, with an accompanying narrative of the students' interactions.

A FAMILY'S "FEUD"

BACKGROUND:

The Ruffin Family includes Mom (Olivia) and Dad (Sanford) and four children: Rachael (age 11), Silvia (age 10), Edmund (age 12), and Rayford (age 14). The family has lived for years in Edison, Illinois. Each summer when the family has traveled on vacation, Mr. and Mrs. Ruffin have decided the travel destination. Guided by the goal to provide everyone with the most wholesome and educational experience, these parents decided where the family should travel and how they should travel. Since the parents were the obvious leaders and had the most authority, they determined the travel plans with no consultation or outward resistance from the children . . . until now. This year Mom and Dad have invited their children to argue for a specific vacation destination, hoping that the conversation about the choices will allow the family to pick the destination that offers the most inclusive appeal.

While Mom and Dad have imagined a vacation destination and activities for the whole family, each of the children has his or her own plan. At a family meeting, each person will have an opportunity to offer a rationale for the plan. Each member of the class needs to be able to represent fairly and accurately the plan of each family member.

In the end, the written analysis will report each family member's plan, and everyone will wrestle with this question: Who gets to decide the vacation plan? Should the adult authorities decide? Should each plan be honored in some way? Can the family reach a compromise? In the end, what seems to be the most reasonable compromise, if one is possible?

LIMITATIONS AND CONSIDERATIONS:

- The family vacation cannot be more than *10 days.*
- The family budget will allow for the cost of no more than *$375.00 per day.*
- Last year the family traveled to Colorado National Monument, near Grand Junction. The family camped in the area. They also visited Arches National Park in Utah. During their stay, they hiked, climbed, rode bikes, fished, and visited historic sites.
- Two years ago, the family traveled to Assateague Island National Seashore in Maryland. The island is famous for its scenic beauty and for its herds of wild horses. On the island, the family visited beaches, took nature walks, fished, shopped, and attended lectures and demonstrations at the island's Visitors' Center.
- If the family travels by car, they are likely to rely on their seven-passenger minivan. The vehicle is 3 years old, and the Ruffins have a car-top carrier to store some luggage.
- Silvia has had some problems with bouts of car sickness in the past, but she may have grown out of this problem. It seems to help if she can ride in the front passenger seat.

OVERVIEW OF THE DECISION-MAKING PROCESS

Since Olivia and Sanford Ruffin are thoughtful parents and want to model for their children that thoughtful people can resolve conflicts through reasoned discussion, they have planned a process for working toward an agreeable solution to the vacation problem. Here are the steps:

STAGE 1:

1. Each group of three to five students will represent a member of the family (the parents will function as a single unit). See the Family Perspectives section beginning on page 69.
2. Each group will study the profile of the family member and the description of his or her preferred vacation destination. Each member of the group should be able to summarize the profile and description so that, when called upon, the speaker can explain to the rest of the class the appeal of the preferred destination.
3. The teacher will serve as the moderator for the family meeting.
4. The teacher will call on one team member to begin the discussion by reporting what the family member prefers. The teacher will record notes on the board, document reader, or video screen, and everyone in the class should write his or her own notes to summarize. *Note: It is necessary, then, for each student to have paper available for recording notes.*

5. After the first speaker reports, each speaker who follows will summarize the previous speaker, evaluate the recommendation, and then report his or her own preference.

6. Throughout the reporting process, everyone should be taking notes in order to be able to report what each speaker said. *Time should be available at the end of this stage for each student to write summaries.*

STAGE 2:

1. After all of the recommendations have been heard, everyone is invited to evaluate them. Which vacation destinations seem best? Which destinations seem less attractive? The students should describe the standard used to judge a destination's quality.

2. While contributing to the debate about the best vacation spot, students should continue to summarize the previous speaker and evaluate whether the suggestions were good or bad.

STAGE 3:

1. The teacher will reorganize groups so that each group has a mixture of perspectives (i.e., different family members).

2. The teacher can offer these directions: "Your new group will imagine themselves as a family counselor. Now that you have experienced the conflict and disagreement among the family members, *prepare a solution to their problem.* Remember that the best solutions would be the ones that respect the interests and the needs of the greatest number of family members."

3. A member from each group will be selected to offer a resolution for the whole class to consider: Given that each family member cannot go on a separate vacation, how should the family resolve its conflict?

4. After students have heard all of the recommendations for resolving the conflict in the Ruffin family, they *summarize the general rules* for working out conflicts when several people disagree about what to do and have distinct points of view. *The teacher at this point would record notes on the board or at the document reader to list the rules. The students should, in turn, expand the notes into coherent sentences to analyze the situation.*

YOUR WRITTEN RESPONSE

Imagine that you are the counselor who is helping the family. Write to the family about their problem, but don't talk about yourself. Your writing should take the form of a report and *not* a letter. Your report should have the following parts:

*   Introduce the report by reminding the family about the basic problem that they face. Reassure the family that the report will offer them advice.

- In a *series of paragraphs*, summarize what each family member wants to do on vacation and explain why he or she wants to do it. Rely on your notes to complete this part.

- Advise the family about the way that they should resolve their current conflict and note the rules that anyone should follow in trying to work out such problems. You have weighed the appeals and shortcomings of each destination and can offer a recommendation that is likely to honor everyone's interests, to an extent. Refer to your notes to develop this part.

THE PROCESS:

- Build on your notes and on your recall of discussions to write a draft of your report.

- Share your draft with a classmate. Your reader should check that the introduction explains the problem, that your summaries are complete and accurate, that your advice is reasonable and complete, and that your writing is carefully edited.

- Guided by your reader's comments, revise the report into a finished product.

FAMILY PERSPECTIVES

OLIVIA AND SANFORD RUFFIN (MOM AND DAD)

Mr. and Mrs. Ruffin are not presenting this trip merely because it is one they would enjoy themselves. They honestly believe their children could benefit from such a trip. Both parents recently have been affected by a book Mrs. Ruffin has read called *Last Child in the Woods*. The Ruffins are concerned that their children are influenced too much by the material world and have not developed enough of an appreciation for the natural world, despite previous trips of this kind. Her husband agrees. Having grown up near the woods in northern Michigan, he spent his youth hunting squirrels, fishing, climbing trees, and generally exploring and enjoying the outdoors. He fears that his children are much too immersed in the modern world of computers, machinery, and cityscapes, and need to spend more time adventuring, exploring, and, in particular, *contemplating* the natural world. Both parents are also hopeful of a renewed interest in American history through exposure to sites pertinent to westward expansion.

The car trip that the parents propose would feature the following highlights: brief stops in Mitchell (Corn Palace) and Deadwood (restoration of Mt. Moriah Cemetery, where Wild Bill Hickok and Calamity Jane are buried); Yellowstone—exploration of geothermal features of the park and night hikes to explore the constellations; Grand Tetons—hikes, horseback riding, and canoeing, which would include exploration of the glacial Lakes; and a trip to Custer Battlefield National Monument.

RACHAEL

Eleven-year-old Rachael has been an enthusiastic and skilled soccer player since she began playing in 1st grade. She now plays with a traveling club soccer team, and she would love to make a career of soccer. Rachael knows that one way to become a better player is to watch the best players as they compete. Rachael knows that the family can't spend the whole vacation watching soccer, but she does hope that they can incorporate soccer as a major part of the plan.

Rachael proposes that the family travel to Cleveland, Ohio. For Rachael, the main attraction would be attendance at two soccer matches. She has learned that this summer, four great teams from Europe will be appearing in U.S. cities for exhibition matches. If Rachael's family visits Cleveland, she can see Glasgow Ranger compete against Glasgow Celtic, and Real Madrid against AC Milan. Attending the matches would be fun for the whole family. Cleveland also offers the Rock and Roll Hall of Fame, the Cleveland Museum of Natural History, and the West Side Market (unusual shops and food stalls). A short distance from Cleveland is the Cedar Point Amusement Park, home of the world's largest roller coaster. Near Cedar Point there is abundant camping, with many outdoor activities possible.

SILVIA

Ten-year-old Silvia is fascinated with celebrities from the entertainment industry. She admires the young actors she sees on television and in movies. She tries to model her appearance after some of the younger actors she sees on television. Of course, that means an investment in the right clothes, grooming, and accessories. Although Silvia's first choice for a vacation would be to visit Hollywood and Beverly Hills, she is willing to take a more modest trip. She knows that her sister and brothers think that she is spoiled because she is the youngest; so for this year's vacation choice, she is willing to compromise, within reason.

She wants to go to Mall of America, in Minneapolis, Minnesota. From Silvia's perspective, Mall of America has a lot for everyone to do. The mall has over 400 stores. There should be stores to attract the interest of everyone in the family. Her sister and brothers can buy new school clothes. The mall also has an amusement park with more than 30 rides, including the ripsaw roller coaster and the Paul Bunyan log chute. There are abundant restaurants and nearby motels. The drive to Minneapolis is relatively short, which means there will be less travel stress and more time for relaxation.

EDMUND

Edmund loves to join his friends on amusement park thrill rides, and he savors adventure movies on DVDs or in the theater. He is also fascinated by aircraft, flight, and space exploration. He most enjoys aerospace activities, like going with his father to the EAA (Experimental Aircraft Association) show each July in Oshkosh, Wisconsin. Whereas his sister Rachael and brother Rayford talk for hours about their sporting events, and Silvia describes in intricate detail her shopping trips, Edmund imagines himself as Chuck Yeager, the first pilot to fly faster than the speed of sound. On frequent evenings, family members find him in his room gazing through his telescope at stars or programming actions for his self-made Lego robots to perform.

Although Edmund usually enjoys the nature trips his parents plan for the family, this year he is hoping to convince everyone to vacation near Orlando, Florida, so that he can use a scholarship he earned through his school's Science Club to attend Kennedy Space Center Camp in mid-June. At camp, he will meet a real astronaut and participate in the Apollo Team to design a space vehicle for exploration and experience what it is like to work and live in space. He knows that his sisters and brother will want to be active and be around children their own ages. Disney World, Universal Studio, and Discovery Cove are only about 45 minutes away for fun and action. Sea World and many nature parks nearby offer more quiet activities. Big Tree Park has a 3,500-year-old bald cypress tree. Lake Louisa State Park offers hiking and horseback riding. Edmund is willing to beg his family and promise to do anything for them for 6 months, if they just go along with him on this vacation plan.

RAYFORD

Fourteen-year-old Rayford will be entering high school in the fall. At this point in his life, he especially values spending time with friends. Sometimes the demands to spend time with family conflict with his need to be with his friends. He is easily bored with family outings that require him to participate in activities that his brother and sisters like but he doesn't like. Rayford likes to participate in sports and likes to be active, especially when activities involve friends. For example, he is looking forward to joining his friends at basketball camp later in the summer.

Rayford's vacation preference is to visit Myrtle Beach, South Carolina. Rayford's friend Dennis spends a good portion of the summer in Myrtle Beach, where Dennis's family has a vacation home. Rayford anticipates that he would be able to spend time with Dennis and with Dennis's South Carolina friends. From conversations with Dennis, Rayford has learned that Myrtle Beach offers many attractions for active teenagers, including amusement parks, beaches, water parks, and shopping malls. In fact, there would be a lot of attractions for everyone in the family. The distance between Edison, Illinois, and Myrtle Beach (950 miles) would make it necessary to take 2 days to drive there. Myrtle Beach has abundant motels, restaurants, and shops.

DISCUSSING THE FAMILY FEUD

In each classroom, after each teacher introduced the problem and described the procedures for deliberation, the students formed small groups and worked on summarizing the argument from the point of view of an assigned character. In each group, following the teacher's model, the students identified key words in the character's written position and relied on these key words to guide their expression of the character's recommendation and rationale. The teachers then reorganized the groups so that each family member's position was represented in each reconstituted group. In the new groups, the students took turns in sharing a family member's argument, following a process that required each speaker to paraphrase the previous speaker's comments before continuing. After the students had heard the summary of each position, they discussed what seemed to be the best destination and the means for selecting a vacation spot that would offer advantages to each member of the family and not penalize anyone.

The small-group discussion led to a whole-class discussion about the students' recommendation for a family vacation destination. The students were not obligated to represent any family member's wishes, but evaluated the several choices to argue for one place that seemed the best fit for the family's interests and for their financial limits and time constraints. Not everyone agreed, so students had to respond to others' assessments of the best places. The process required the students to review each choice and look for a destination that would suit everyone to some extent. Following the teacher's prompt and modeling, the students were able to write to the family to offer advice. Most important for the work that would follow, the students were able to advance a solution that honored the interests and needs of all the family members, without elevating one person's wishes above everyone else's. Moving forward, the teachers felt confident that the students could deliberate civilly about complex problems, relying on their work with basic elements of argument and drawing from their experience as negotiators for a reasonable compromise.

EXPRESSING A QUALITY STANDARD FOR WRITING

The two 5th-grade teachers I have studied wanted to position students to be able to talk about the quality of their own written work and the work of their classmates. One teacher, Ms. Wieczorek, observed: "If we want students to write high-quality compositions, they would need to have in mind what a good composition looks like and sounds like. We encourage students to work through drafts and continue to revise and refine their work. In order to do that, the students need to know something about the qualities of good writing. And if they are going to talk to one another about how they might improve their work, they should have in mind a common idea of what good writing is."

The teachers report that they typically follow one of two approaches to help students express a quality standard for the specific kind of writing that they will be doing. When the teachers have examples of student writing of the sort that the class is expected to produce, they invite the students to discuss in groups their understanding of the common features of the writing and their rankings of the relative quality of the compositions. If the teachers do not have examples of student work, or if they do not have permission to use the examples, they construct their own samples. The teachers judge that it is best to give students examples that represent a range of writing quality. When the students work with the sample compositions, they discuss two questions: (1) What do all of these examples have in common? (2) How would we rank the compositions for quality, from best to worst? The discussion about these two questions allows the students to note the key features that distinguish the particular genre (what they have in common), and to express the features that the students find particularly appealing (talking about what they like and don't like) in the set of compositions. At other points in the composing process, the students can reference these features and qualities as they talk to one another or to the teacher about what they are trying to accomplish and how they can improve their work.

The second option for the teachers is to invite students to talk more generally about what they expect to see in good writing. A question such as the following prompts the discussion: "Now that you know what everyone will be writing, what would you expect to see in very good writing of this kind?" The teachers report that in 5th grade the students speak globally about good writing, using such descriptors as these: flows, keeps your interest, stays on track, long enough but not too long, organized, and so forth. During the discussions, the teachers help with the language to express these qualities; for example, *flow* becomes something like this: "The sentences and paragraphs connect with one another in an obvious way." This preliminary process, then, helps the students to construct a quality standard—not one that looks like a multicolumn rubric that describes levels of performance, but an expression of the features of the best writing of the sort that the students are trying to produce.

DEFINING AND MODELING THE WRITING TASK

The two writing prompts that appear in Chapter 3 are rather complex, especially for a group of 5th-graders. The teachers not only helped students to understand the language of the prompts and the reader's expectations associated with them (e.g., what a principal would need to know, what a legislator would need to know), but they needed to demonstrate procedures for planning and composing.

It is one thing to explain to students what they should do, and another matter to model for students a process that a writer might follow in attempting to address a particular problem for a specific audience. In the case of the problem with the middle school bullies, the teacher would draw from students' suggestions and compose at the overhead projector or document reader. Following the example of one teacher, Ms. Boski, the interchange could look something like this:

Ms. Boski: The principal is a very busy person, with lots of problems on his mind. What does he need to know about the situation that we have been discussing?

Millie: That these two kids are bullies.

Ms. Boski: I think he will need to know something more specific than that. What is the *specific* situation? Why is it a problem for the principal to think about?

Carl: He has to do something about it.

Ms. Boski: About what? We still haven't said, specifically, what the problem is.

Louise: This brother and sister . . .

Franco: Leila and Landon. I remember.

Louise: This brother and sister—Leila and Landon—have been picking on this other kid, Jimmy.

Ms. Boski: OK, so (writing displayed on the projector screen) *I know that you have been troubled by the behavior of two students—Leila and Landon Kramden. They have admitted to harming Jimmy Farfel in a number of ways, and you need to find a way to repair the harm to Jimmy.* OK, so far I have reminded the principal about the events and about the problem he faces in deciding what to do. So, what can you say to him?

Louise: They should be punished.

Ms. Boski: In what way? Like kicking them out of school?

Sharon: No. We decided that they should say they're sorry and pay him back. We also said they should do like a service project.

Ms. Boski (writing for display): *Leila and Landon should take a few simple steps to repair the harm they have caused Jimmy.*

Ms. Boski then reads the newly composed introduction aloud and asks the students whether they find it satisfactory. She does not leave the composition on display for students to copy. To her mind, the important element is the thinking aloud about the composing process, and she does not want her work simply to be imitated. Instead, she would like each student to follow through with a similar composing process, thinking about how to introduce the central problem, or area of inquiry, for an audience and taking a position in response to the problem. Ms. Boski noted, "The kids need to be able to read and talk about the writing examples in order to identify important and necessary elements of the writing genre. They can then work to incorporate these elements in their writing." She wants students to have command of the language for talking about the qualities of writing and not simply imitate someone else's example.

PLANNING AND DRAFTING

In some instances the 5th-grade teachers provide students with a graphic organizer, usually in the form of a list of requirements suggested by the prompt, and accompanying spaces for writing notes related to these requirements. At the same time, the teachers recognize that all writers do not plan in the same way; in fact, it appears that some writers begin to compose without putting a formal plan down on paper, especially when word processing makes it relatively easy to forge ahead with a draft. So the teachers demonstrate a couple of possibilities for planning, choosing from these options: informal list or formal outline, graphic display like a tree diagram or web, or drawings and notes.

From their plans, the students execute drafts of a written response. Since drafting is a recursive rather than a linear process, the students again can take advantage of discussions with peers to check that they are on the right track, based on their own rubric, and to ensure that the composition is generally clear and organized. The teachers intervene frequently with specific students who are eager to share their writing and with those who seek help.

Although the classes of 5th-graders worked to develop their own rubric for judging the quality of their writing, the teachers did not follow these rubrics rigidly to assign grades to the compositions. First, the class' evaluation criteria served as a common standard and familiar language for the teachers to offer feedback on the students' writing. Following the structured process that the teachers had designed, the students predictably wrote compositions that exhibited the features listed in the rubric. The teachers also took into account the growth of the individual students, some of whom had active learning plans that identified specific language challenges. In short, the teachers were not concerned that they were contributing to grade inflation. According to Ms. Wieczorek, "Someone might look at the grades in here and think that we are being too liberal. But our kids write incredible compositions and grow so much during the year. It is all about the growth and not about how many As and Bs appear in our gradebooks."

REVISING, EDITING, AND ASSESSING

At various points in the composing process, the students check the quality of their work. They read what they have written, checking for the sound, the "flow," the "correctness," and the alignment with the requirements. It would be a rare student who wrote a complete composition and waited until the entire draft was complete before checking possibilities for editing and revising. Students seek assistance often, sometimes relying on peers and sometimes conferring with the teacher.

The 5th-grade teachers are less concerned about the students being "correct" in their execution of a written analysis than they are about the quality of students' critical evaluation and elaborated arguments. The teachers acknowledge the influence of Smith and Wilhelm (2007) and Weaver (1996) as they focus on a handful of key usage concepts and language conventions. Ms. Boski said, "The district's literacy curriculum specifies the concepts that we are supposed to be teaching, but sometimes the sequence doesn't line up with the kind of writing the students are doing." Ms. Wieczorek observed: "Generally, we do two things: When we have samples of what students write, we look for patterns of difficulties. You can expect some misspelled words, especially if the students are tackling a new issue in their writing, like the reparations problem. The spelling doesn't seem to be a big issue. I mean, the misspellings are not so gross that a reasonable person couldn't figure out what they mean. But we worry a bit more when students write the whole composition as one or two long sentences, or don't seem to know where to begin a new paragraph. The other thing we try to do is anticipate the specific grammar or punctuation ideas that kids should know for a particular kind of writing. For example, in writing to a legislator or to the principal, the students needed to know some conventions for a formal letter. They weren't writing a text to a friend, so there is a way to introduce the subject and a certain language that is appropriate. It is more about problem solving than memorizing rules."

So editing is part of the process, and the teachers model the editing, just as they modeled the planning and drafting. In general, they promote the use of active voice, they ask students to check for clarity in pronoun reference, and they encourage precision in choosing words appropriate for the given audience and purpose.

FOLLOWING A STRUCTURED PROCESS

This chapter and the previous one describe the overall process of helping students to learn procedures for composing elaborated responses to complex problems. While Chapter 3 emphasizes the exploratory and preparatory discussions that precede the writing, this chapter acknowledges that the inquiry begins with learning the tools for argument and discussion, and extends into students' attempts at writing logical, coherent, and elaborated responses. The follow-through includes the construction and iteration of a quality standard that will guide the production and review of the specific form of writing. Students apply procedures from oral discourse—advancing arguments, paraphrasing the arguments of others, summarizing a sequence of arguments, weighing one perspective against another, and so on—to their written responses. The teacher's modeling of planning and composing processes supports the students' attempts. The students' efforts to produce written responses extend from their planning and drafting. As a common practice for review throughout the process, the students share drafts with one another and with the teacher, referencing all along the quality standards or assessment criteria that the learners helped to establish during small-group and whole-class discussion at the initiation of the sequence.

The 5th-grade teachers both noted that they occasionally ask students to write a brief reflection to explain to someone else how they were able to produce the composition they had just completed. The idea is that they would like the learners to be aware of the processes that they followed to write a composition. Ms. Boski acknowledged, "We know that this would be a good practice after almost all compositions, especially if the students are writing something new. But there never seems to be enough time. We follow pacing guides that suggest that we have to move quickly on to a new unit." But she also found students' reflections revealing: "At the end of the year the students were asked to reflect on their writing, including what they found most helpful when composing a written response. The over-whelming response was that it was very helpful to talk through the scenario about which they would be writing. They would get ideas from one another. Additionally, other students would comment on their ideas, which helped to validate or refine their opinions and thoughts on a subject."

Inquiry drives the entire process described in this and the previous chapter, and the authentic discussions among the students contribute much to their being able to produce elaborated and logical written arguments. The discussions situate students to engage in procedures for argument and analysis. When many students express their assessments, offering examples and citing warrants, they contribute substantive knowledge to the whole class. The skeptics and critics serve an important function, as they question the accuracy and relevance of examples and test the warrants used to interpret examples. The dynamic environment in which there can be respectful disagreement promotes purposeful interactions and immerses learners in procedures that are important generally in thinking about critical issues, in conversing in a constructive way with peers and adults, and in writing to advance a proposition in the context of competing positions and acknowledged doubt. The next chapter follows a class of 9th-graders closely as they engage in a sequence of carefully orchestrated and linked discussions that the teacher intends to prepare the students for writing an essay and for reading a novel critically.

CHAPTER 5

A Cycle of Discussion and Inquiry

My classroom observations and collaborations over the past 7 years have included work with the team of 5th-grade teachers featured in the previous two chapters, with three high school English teachers, and with a community college teacher. I was especially interested in looking into their classrooms because these teachers expressed their intent to teach in an inquiry-based way, and they noted that they valued authentic discussion as a key element in an inquiry process. Recognizing that Nystrand's (1997) research reveals that authentic discussion is rare, I acknowledge that the teachers whom I observed and interviewed were far from representative of teachers in general. I also acknowledge that the teachers worked under rather favorable conditions, in schools that had sufficient resources, where parents were supportive, and where learners were generally enthusiastic and cooperative. But the practices that these teachers followed do not require abundant resources or supportive parents; the teachers found replicable ways to initiate and sustain inquiry and discussion to prepare students to write and to develop command of the procedures for critical thinking and composing.

In this chapter I focus attention on one 9th-grade English teacher. She teaches in a "high-performing" school, with students who come from middle-class and upper-middle-class homes. It is important to note this specific context, because the teacher's practices as a designer and initiator of inquiry and as facilitator and manager of discussions may not be appropriate for every student population. At the same time, most teachers would likely benefit from following many of the teacher's practices in planning for discussions, in linking them together, in facilitating large-group discussions and managing small-group work, and in building one discussion upon another in an inquiry progression. The 9th-grade teacher, Ms. Edsel, who is featured in the next chapter as well, relied on a simple device to tap prior knowledge and introduce students to the focus for shared inquiry. She designed structured forums in which the learners could talk in a purposeful way, specifying intended outcomes and parameters for talking. She built one discussion upon another to advance students' understanding and refine their thinking and the language with which they discussed complex concepts.

I observed the teacher during three lessons, on alternate days, and discussed with the teacher the activities from the days when I could not visit the class. I focus, then, on a sequence of five class meetings. I draw from interviews with the teacher to project the further application of procedures developed during the discussions I observed. My observations of this one teacher revealed to me two rather obvious conclusions: (1) All discussions are not the same; they do not all serve the same function; and (2) the nature of discussions depends on the structures and expectations that the teacher, as the orchestrator for learning, establishes. Taken together, these two observations suggest that for the strategic teacher, discussions are not isolated intellectual moments, but are part of a larger cycle intended to advance deep understandings and important proficiencies for problem solving, social interaction, and written composition.

I hope to illustrate these two conclusions by showing the students in action during small-group work and in whole-class discussions. The teacher prompts the discussions with two different inquiry-based activities. As the activity changes, and as the phase of the activity changes, the students' discussion changes, but it builds on itself. With the help of research assistants, I have coded the discussions to quantify the students' discourse moves. The series of graphs that summarize the discourse contributions in each discussion illustrate the contrasts among discussions, and I hope that the graphic representations reveal the different functions of the discussions and the scaffolding effect that shows how one discussion depended on the previous one.

DISCUSSION AND LEARNING
SOME PROCEDURES FOR DEFINING

The 9th-grade teacher, Ms. Edsel, introduced a unit of instruction by noting that the students ultimately would be working with some literature in which the authors seem to imply that all human beings have an obligation to help their fellow human beings. Noting current political debates, Ms. Edsel observed that many thinkers test the assumption of obligations to serve others, seeing this obligation as an impingement on personal liberty. She noted that the class would begin by attempting to define the notion of *obligation*, as the term is used in appeals to help fellow human beings, and to rely on the defining criteria that the students might develop to evaluate the behavior of characters in fiction and to appraise the implications of the authors' narratives. Ms. Edsel then initiated the inquiry with the following survey, which the students first completed individually and then brought to their small-group discussions in groups of three or four students.

SURVEY: WHAT IS YOUR OBLIGATION TO OTHERS?

Directions: Read each of the following statements and circle the extent to which you agree or disagree with the statement, using the following scale:

  4 = strongly agree
  3 = agree
  2 = disagree
  1 = strongly disagree
  0 = not sure

Be as candid as possible. Support each of your responses with an example from popular culture, personal life, news stories, literature, etc. Then write a rule that supports the position you take.

1. I am my brother's keeper.
2. Being a best friend means that you always have your friend's back, no matter what.
3. When a child misbehaves, it is the parents who are at fault.
4. It is OK to use friends to your advantage, but only if one gets something out of the relationship as well.
5. Friends should always wish for the best for one another.
6. In school, when students work in small groups, they are responsible for the work of their fellow group members.
7. Blood is thicker than water.
8. The boss should be friends with his or her employees.
9. Teachers should always get to know their students' likes and dislikes.
10. If you are friends with someone on Facebook, you always have to wish that person "happy birthday" on his or her birthday.

The following exchange represents a typical portion of conversation among students across the class as they reacted to the set of statements in the survey. Although Ms. Edsel did not designate a group member as the discussion facilitator, one student assumed the lead to begin the conversation, and the discussion progressed from her initial reporting of her judgment about the first statement.

Adrian: OK . . . so, the first one is "I am my brother's keeper," and what I said was it depends whether you're younger or older, because typically, if you're younger, then you'll look up to your older siblings, almost as a parental figure, because they have more experience than you.

Bob: So, what did you say, though? Like agree, not sure . . . ?

Adrian: I said, agree if you're older, and, uh, um, younger is, it's not as much, so I say semi-agree [laughs], if you know what I mean. Because it's kinda like, you look up to your younger, like, your younger brother, but, um, I mean, if you're younger, you don't really take care of your older siblings. I mean . . .

Kanji: I mean, you can, if you're old enough and are able to.

Bob: Yeah, or, or if they need the help, and, like, if they're not, like, I guess physically able in this situation or mentally able, then you're sort of in a position where you have to be their keeper, in order for them to sort of, like . . .

Kanji: It's very situational.

Bob: Yeah, yeah, that's why I put down more of a not sure than . . .

Kanji: [indistinct] I put agree.

Adrian: Yeah, I said agree, too.

Bob: For the most part it's agree, but . . .

Kanji: The second one . . .

Adrian: Oh, we have to give an example, too.

Bob: OK, I don't think . . .

Adrian: I said *My Sister's Keeper*, the movie.

Kanji: That's what I was thinking, too.

Bob: That's what I was thinking, not that I read it or watched it, not that that it has something to do with my sex or anything, but, um, I, like, a bunch of girls talked about it in like 5th grade, and they told me about it, and I guess I thought about that example.

Adrian: Well, technically, because the girl is younger . . .

Others: Yeah.

Adrian: When you think about it . . .

Kanji: That makes sense.

Adrian: So I kind of agree with it.

Bob: Or almost like . . .

Adrian: I don't know if I strongly agree, but I say I agreed with it.

Kanji: Yeah. I have an example. I don't know if, you guys probably haven't seen the show, but I watch *The Carrie Diaries*, and, yeah, but the little sister, because their mom died, the little sister, she's, like, really getting taken care of by her older sister.

Adrian: Even in, like, *I-Carly*, her brother, like, looks after her.

Kanji: So it's kind of like in television and in pop culture and it kind of shows that siblings do take care of each other.

Bob: Yeah, I remember reading . . .

Kanji: Yeah, we should go on to the next one, sorry.

Adrian: [indecipherable] . . . that friends should have your friend's back no
    matter what?
Bob: I'm leaning towards not sure, towards disagree.
Kanji: Really?
Bob: It, it really, like you said before, it depends on the situation, like, if
    your friend's the kind of guy that gets into fights a lot, then, I mean,
    why would you have his back if he's causing a bit of, um, trouble?
Kanji: Well, I was thinking, like, if you're best . . . there's a reason you're
    best friends. You're best friends, you should be having each other's . . .
Bob: Yeah, but I think it's not for every single situation, because they could
    be getting into things that you're not, you shouldn't be involved in,
    and . . .
Kanji: Then, do you really wanna be their best friend? I mean . . .
Bob: Well, that's . . .
Adrian: Well, an example is *Friends*. That came to my mind, because
    they're always there for each other no matter what, like they get into
    crazy situations . . .
Kanji: Yeah.

The discussion above represents what Barnes (1992, 2008) and Smagorinsky (2007) call *exploratory talk*. Perhaps the sequence of discussions, even
as they become a bit more refined and complex, remain exploratory; but this
initial phase of the sequence reveals the students in discovering the positions
held by the members of the group. The conversation is a kind of sharing
and groping, with students initially expressing uncertainty about their own
positions and the positions of their partners. Prompted by the teacher, the
small-group members move on to identifying examples of situations that
would support the positions they hold. They cite brief narratives from movies or television programs and explain how the narratives influence their
judgments or illustrate their decisions. As the conversation progresses, the
students affirm, question, or qualify the conclusions expressed by partners.
For example, the group appears to agree that one has a responsibility to support a friend, unless that friend consistently gets into trouble that also might
compromise the supportive friend.

In the small-group discussion, not only are the students engaged in the
procedures for asserting claims, supporting the claims with examples, and
explaining those examples, but they also are refining their conclusions. The
process appears to be leading to the expression of a set of rules or warrants
that will be useful in subsequent discussions when the students share their
prepared analysis with the entire class, in a forum that will invite others to
cite different examples and perhaps express different warrants.

PUTTING ARGUMENTS TOGETHER

After the students had spent approximately 25 minutes in small-group discussion about the survey items, the teacher called the class to come together to share their conclusions and analyses. The following excerpt from that exchange represents the kind of exchanges that occurred in the large-group forum. While the talk continues to be exploratory, the students move to another level of refinement of their thinking. Each student's conversational turn is longer than the typical turns in the small-group discussions, and the teacher plays a more assertive role as facilitator.

Ms. Edsel: So, over the course of the next, you know, 2 to 3 weeks, we'll be looking at this notion of *obligation*. What we're going do now is share some of the arguments or situations with the class, and I do suggest that on the back of the sheet, you take some notes, to define obligation, or to define questions we're uncertain about, for establishing different relationships that related to obligation. So as we're going through this, it's probably a good idea to take notes, because you'll reflect on these notes as we move forward in the inquiry. So, does some group or one person want to start with either something they're really certain of? Something where you put just "not agree."

Haley: OK, can I start with any of these?

Ms. Edsel: Any of them.

Haley: OK. So I wanna start with the one about whether the boss should be friends with his or her employees, because I think this is the one that I, like, knew my, like, opinion on the most. So I said disagree, because, um, I'm going to give an example of the show *The Office*; in *The Office*, half of the employees never get their work done because they're too busy having fun, and the bosses can't yell at them because they don't wanna be bad friends. So, if you think about it, um, if someone's trying to be friends with someone, like, in a workplace, they lose, like, that authority figure, and they go into kind of more of like a friend figure, and they can't have any, um, any respect for them anymore. So you really need to have those roles set straight. So I said disagree.

Mike: Going along with her point, I also said disagree, and I wrote the show, my example is George Lopez, because he's like the boss of the comp-, of the place, and he, and his friends work there, and he doesn't let them get fired in many episodes, even though they're not good workers and stuff . . . [indecipherable]

Haley: I agree with you, because if the boss becomes friends with his workers, then their workers will slack off, thinking their job is secure because their friend is the boss. And also, it would be really hard to fire somebody that was your friend.

Bob: So I agree with all of you to disagree. And I also took it not just as a matter of respect and a matter of firing your friends; I also took it in the sense that the point of your job and your workplace is to get things done, and to actually continue production or to continue your job, and in this situation, like we said with *The Office*, if the boss was friends with his or her employees, then it would slow down production and it would slow down whatever you're trying to do, and that's kind of the purpose of a workplace, to be doing what you have to do in order to get paid, and this would completely, just, like, alter it. And a boss doesn't have to be friends with his or her employees. Like, they can choose to do whatever they want. It's not a *should be* or a *have to be*; it's just a *want to be*.

Eleanor: I said agree, because in the movie *Horrible Bosses*, the employee and the boss are, like, enemies; they, like, hate each other. And then, like, it ended up with, like, the employee quitting because they're, like, so hard to get along with. So I think sometimes it's a good thing to be friends with your boss.

Samantha: I . . . well, when I was reading it, I said not sure, because I asked a question, like, will it affect each other's work habits, and I think it, like, depends, like, if they're able to, like, still work in wherever they are, then it should be OK, because it's always good, to, like, be able to talk to, like, someone. But if it's gonna affect how they work and how the finished product ends up, then I think it's not OK.

Ms. Edsel: So you think we need to ask the question, Samantha, does it affect the work habit, and then make a decision?

Leticia: I agree with that, and, like, along with Bob's point, I'd move it to, teachers should get to know their students' likes and dislikes, like, along the same line. It's a teacher's job to teach, but it's not their responsibility to have a personal . . . well, they can have a personal relationship, but it's not like they must. Their main focus should be teaching, just like the boss and their employees, their main focus should be work. And if a friendship comes along from that, that's OK, but it's not, like, required.

Cassie: Going back to Eleanor's point, I disagree with her point, because in the movie they were enemies, but it doesn't say in this statement, it doesn't say, like, that the boss, if the boss isn't friends with them that they have to be enemies. They just have to be neutral with each other. Michael . . .

Michael: I actually agree with what he said, too, but I think it's more, like, it's more on the obligation of the employee to be friends with the boss, but it isn't the boss' obligation to be friends with the employee.

Ms. Edsel: So you think, so you're saying that it's the boss', it's the employee's obligation to be friendly to the boss, but it's not kind of the boss' obligation to kind of create a relationship with . . . . Why do you say that?

Michael: Because the, the employee has to . . . the employee works for the boss, the boss is, is, he's the employer, so he, basically he gets the say on [indecipherable] fire people [indecipherable] king–servant relationship . . .

Ms. Edsel: A king–servant relationship.

Bob: So you're saying it's OK to suck up, but it's not OK to be friends with people who are below you?

Michael: No, you're not obligated to. He can do that, but he doesn't have to.

Bob: When have you ever heard of a situation where a king couldn't be friends with a servant because he's not obligated to, though?

Michael: Exactly.

[indecipherable whispering and cross-talk]

Ms. Edsel: Guys.

Michael: Because most of the time, the boss has, like, another boss, so if he, like, expects his boss to be, like, friendly with him, then he should also be friendly with his, like, workers, like, under him.

Adrian: So this, because this, I think you also, one of you said about how a teacher should also get to know their students' likes and dislikes, it goes right with that, I think, because, I think school and work is about putting aside social interests, and just teaching the students or doing a job, because you don't get hired for a job to be friends with people. It's that line, you know, that quotation, um, "Let's make this a purely, um, professional relationship." That's how it should always be in school and work, because it's really not a social environment, so, that's what I have.

Allen: Going back to Bob's point, you said that, um, a king can't have a relationship with a servant.

Bob: I said he wasn't obligated to. No, no, no, wait . . . you said . . . never mind.

Allen: I think, remember, you said that . . . Michael said that he could have it but he wasn't obligated to, but you said have you ever heard of a king being friends with a servant?

Bob: Yes.

Allen: Well, what about the TV show *Merlin*?

I have observed hundreds of hours of classroom instruction, and rarely have I seen discussion of this sort. I am struck first by the length of the contributions. In a sense, the students seem to have worked out their arguments and rehearsed them in the small-group forums. Each contributor comes to the large-group discussion with fully developed arguments—assertions supported by examples, interpreted by invoking a relevant warrant. The teacher had planned purposefully for this sequence so that the students began in small groups by reacting to statements, discovering illustrative examples, and explaining the connections between the examples and the assertions that they support.

The teacher initiates the discussion by noting the purpose for the talk. She encourages the students to take notes because they will later write an extended definition. In other words, she infuses the talk with purpose, and she connects the current discussion to subsequent activities in the sequence of learning. The teacher provides the students with some choice about where to begin the discussion in response to Haley's question, "Can I start with any of these?" The teacher might be the gatekeeper for the contributions, perhaps nodding or pointing to students to select them as speakers, but these cues are not indicated in the recordings. Instead, the students take responsibility themselves for taking turns and responding to one another.

In the large-group discussion, the students practice what Collins (1982), Nystrand (1997), and Applebee, Langer, Nystrand, and Gamoran (2003) call *uptake*: that is, the building on another speaker's contribution to situate and extend the thinking about the topic. Leticia notes, "I agree with that, and, like, along with Bob's point, I'd move it to, teachers should get to know their students' likes and dislikes. . . ." Michael says, "I actually agree with what he said, too, but I think it's more. . . ." Adrian introduces her contribution in this way: ". . . one of you said about how a teacher should also get to know their students' likes and dislikes, it goes right with that. . . ." These examples of uptake are more than the courteous behavior of acknowledging another speaker. They reveal an extension of thinking—that the speaker knows how others are thinking about the question of obligation, that the speaker wants to insert an addition to the previous contributions, and that the speaker will offer a variation or possible refinement of what has already been said, especially since the class is working toward a common understanding or definition of what *obligation* means.

In a sense the small-group work begins with sorting through positions relative to the survey statements, prompting each group member to voice a claim. Then the students work toward citing a relevant example and explaining it. In the large-group discussion, the students come already equipped with their examples and their analysis. The large-group discussion does not reveal students disputing one another about the examples; instead, the students offer alternative examples. If they contest one another, the disagreement focuses on the interpretation of the example: its relevance and its wording. For example, Adrian builds on previous comments to offer a qualified rule: "I think school and work is about putting aside social interests, and just teaching the students or doing a job, because you don't get hired for a job to be friends with people."

While the stated purpose for the sequence of discussions is to define the abstract concept of *obligation*, the definition will require argument, in the sense that the defining strategy includes supporting criterion statements with relevant examples and explaining the connection between the examples and the statements (Hillocks, Kahn, & Johannessen, 1983). In other words, the inquiry process that leads toward a definition requires argument in the sense of units of logical thought. In both the small-group and large-group discussions in Ms. Edsel's class, the 9th-graders practice some procedures for argument, including making claims, supporting them with examples, interpreting the examples with warrants, recognizing rebuttal positions, and evaluating the merits of the rebuttals.

In the large-group discussion, Ms. Edsel manages the conversation, but makes few substantive contributions. She initiates the conversation. Later she paraphrases the speaker's contribution and checks for the accuracy of her representation: "So you think we need to ask the question, Samantha, does it affect the work habit, and then make a decision?" She also prompts the speaker to elaborate in a way that asks for justification for an assertion: "So you think, so you're saying that it's the boss', it's the employee's obligation to be friendly to the boss, but it's not kind of the boss' obligation to kind of create a relationship with. . . . Why do you say that?" Sometimes, Ms. Edsel redirects the conversation when it appears that the students speak over one another and lose their focus.

It is also noteworthy that across the small-group discussions and the large-group discussions, there is almost no apparent social conversation. When a research assistant and I initially coded the transcripts, we thought we had identified one instance over six discussions across three class meetings that we could label as social conversation. There are probably many steps that the teacher took to foster a classroom where students could take responsibility for contributing to discussions in civil and rational ways. At the same time, it appears that at least three factors influenced how students conducted themselves in a purposeful way in small-group and large-group meetings: (1) The teacher connected the current discussion to the broader program of inquiry and to long-term outcomes; (2) the teacher identified a specific purpose for each discussion; and (3) the teacher expressed specific expectations for each discussion, including the length of time for the small-group work and the target outcome for the discussion. These should probably be conventional routines in every classroom, but are seldom attended to with as much care as Ms. Edsel appears to take. I suggest that a teacher's planning class discussions around these routines will provide the foundation for successful interactions of the type observed in Ms. Edsel's class.

COMPLICATING THINKING BEHIND ARGUMENTS

While the class arrived at a preliminary expression of criteria for defining an abstract concept, Ms. Edsel extended the discussion to refine the criterion statements and to test them against specific situations (see Appendix A for the complete set of problem-based scenarios). Ms. Edsel anticipated that the discussion of problem-based scenarios might be new to her 9th-graders, so she began by modeling the discussion of the first scenario and then turned over responsibility to the students in groups of three or four. This practice of modeling and then releasing responsibility to the students is consistent with the practices that Smagorinsky and Fly (1993, 1994) report, with students imitating the behaviors that the teacher models when she facilitates discussion. Specifically, Ms. Edsel modeled how to initiate the discussion, how to encourage participation, how to build on contributions, how to paraphrase, and how to react respectfully to responses. Teachers who seek to make small-group work more productive and meaningful would do well to follow Ms. Edsel's example in practicing her facilitation routines and her careful sequencing of discussion opportunities. In the following excerpt, the teacher prompts the students to begin, and they assume responsibility.

Ms. Edsel: So now what you're going do in your groups for the next 10 to 15 minutes is look at scenarios two, three, and four. Use the graphic organizer to complete . . . so we've got what the problem is, solutions, we've talked about the warrants, and then as you're working through what you are learning about obligation. OK. So now in your groups, two, three, and four, about 10 to 15 minutes, and then we'll share in the big group and we'll do the other. All right, go ahead.

Cassie (reading from the handout): . . . invited and frequently bad-mouthed by Alicia. On the rare occasion that Jenni is invited, and Jenni cannot make it due to family and school conflicts, Alicia calls her a bad friend. This pattern of behavior has gone on for quite some time, but so far Kristi has chosen not to intervene. As time passes, Jenni is becoming more and more upset and hurt, and asks Kristi to do the same, something to Alicia . . . asks Kristi to say something to Alicia, but Kristi still doesn't want to get in the middle of it. What should Kristi do?

Mike: OK, so . . . I think she should, like, talk to Alicia.

Allen: Who? Kristi?

Mike: Kristi.

Cassie: I think, yeah. Because she's bad-mouthing her friend, and it makes her uncomfortable, and she's being a bad friend for making her friend uncomfortable.

Mike: Yeah.

Cassie: So I think she should . . .

Mike: Like, at least tell Alicia not to talk about her friend like that.

Cassie: Like, they don't have to be friends, but they don't have to bad-mouth each other.

Allen: [indistinct] if she should say something to Alicia.

Ms. Edsel (joining the group briefly): Again as you're looking at the scenarios, think of, and analyze all the people in the relationship.

Allen: I think she should say something.

Mike: So the warrant would be, like, one should, like, defend their friends.

Leticia: One should attempt to preserve friendship.

Allen: I don't think Kristi did anything.

Cassie: I think we should say Kristi hasn't . . .

Leticia: But it's, like, her friend that was saying things. It's just that . . .

Allen: Are you responsible for what your friends do?

Leticia: But she's being a bystander.

Cassie: Well, if it makes her uncomfortable, she should say something.

Allen: It doesn't make her uncomfortable.

Cassie: Yeah, it does.

Allen: How do you know?

Mike: Wouldn't you feel uncomfortable?

Allen: [indecipherable]

Cassie: It says as the time passes, Jenni's becoming more and more upset and hurt, and Kristi asks . . . still doesn't say anything, and Kristi doesn't want to get in the middle of it. So that shows that she's uncomfortable.

Allen: Jenni's not friends with Alicia.

Cassie and Mike: Yeah, they both are.

Cassie: She says . . . she doesn't want to get in the middle of it; she'd be uncomfortable getting in the middle of it.

Allen: It means she doesn't care.

Mike: No, it doesn't.

Allen: Look; if you're uncomfortable [indistinct] about something, you kind of, like, stand up for that person, you try to take care of them. You're not just gonna sit there and do nothing.

Mike: No, *uncomfortable* means, like, you don't feel comfortable in a situation, you don't wanna, you wanna back off.

Allen: That's not friends . . . [indecipherable] So that means [indecipherable]

Cassie: [indecipherable] How does this scenario . . . I think obligation, that Kristi has an obligation to be a friend to both of her friends.

Allen: [indecipherable]

Cassie: You write your own thing, then, Michael.
Mike: So, friends have, like, an obligation to, like, protect their friends.
Leticia: A true friend would always have their friend's back.

This is the fourth discussion in a sequence of discussions: small-group discussion of survey statements, whole-class debriefing about the survey discussions, the teacher's modeling of the scenario discussion, and the small-group discussion of a set of scenarios. Again, the last discussion is different from previous discussions. Earlier, the students reacted to the survey statements and derived a tentative list of criteria for defining *obligation*. But when a group of discussants agree to a set of rules or warrants, they may not agree on the application of the rules. The discussion of the scenarios focuses on attempts to refine warrants. In the small-group discussions about the scenarios, the students do not invent examples, because the scenario itself is the example available for illustrating claims. If there are challenges, in the form of questioning or disagreeing, the challenges focus on the warrants. It appears that the small-group discussion extends the students' thinking about the concept of *obligation*, with the participants working toward refinement of their criterion statements. As the students finish discussion of the second scenario, Mike offers this: "So, friends have, like, an obligation to, like, protect their friends." Leticia proposes in return that "a true friend would always have their friend's back."

A PATTERN ACROSS A DISCUSSION SEQUENCE

In the 9th-grade classes that I observed, there were two more steps in the process: the teacher-led, whole-class discussion of some of the scenarios and small-group discussion of the remaining scenarios. In total, then, over three class meetings, the students participated in six discussions. In each case, I audio-recorded the discussion. In the case of the whole-class discussion, I recorded all of the participants. In the case of the small-group discussions, I randomly selected one group to record on each occasion. While I recorded one small group, I could observe all of the groups. The teacher and I agreed that the recorded group was representative of what occurred in each group.

A research assistant transcribed all of the recordings. I developed a system of codes (Appendixes B and C), based on anticipation of the utterances that one was likely to hear in discussions designed to prepare students for writing an extended definition essay. See Appendix B for a description of the method of developing the codes and refining them. Since the length of each discussion varied, I report the data in percentages. Appendix D offers a summary of the percentages across discussions. Figures 5.1–5.6 (pp. 92–93) offer a graphic representation of the differences across six discussions.

While all of the discussions were in a sense *exploratory*, the initial discussion appears to have been a process of revealing the positions of the discussants. In the initial discussion, the students also derived examples to support their judgments and explained to one another how the examples aligned with their judgments. In the subsequent large-group discussion, the contributors offered more fully developed arguments, in the sense of making a claim, citing an example, and explaining the example. It appears that the initial small-group discussion prepared the learners to express arguments fully in the large-group discussion. The large-group discussion exposed the whole class to a variety of arguments, built on a variety of examples. The students did not often contest one another's judgments; instead, they extended the discussion by citing alternative examples and variations on the wording of warrants. With the teacher facilitating the large-group discussion, the students appeared to balance their contributions with the expressing of claims, citing data in the form of examples, and interpreting the data.

In the initial large-group discussion about a scenario, the teacher models the process that she expects the students to follow in their small groups. Since the scenario presents a problem, the students disagree and express some challenges, which are an important part of the process and can be handled civilly. In the small-group discussions about the scenarios, the students rely on the scenario itself as the example to illustrate claims. The students initially disagree a good deal about the action that the character in the scenario should take, especially in contrast to the initial discussion about the survey responses (21.5% of contributions in the scenario discussion vs. 4.0% during the survey discussion). The challenges and disagreements focus mostly on the warrants that students express to interpret the scenario to arrive at a judgment about the character.

The data in Appendix D and represented in Figures 5.1–5.6 reveal that not all of the discussions leading to the writing of an extended definition were the same. Each discussion appears to have served a different function; for example, discovering one's position and the positions of peers, finding examples to support claims, deriving warrants, testing arguments among a group of peers, responding to challenges, and refining arguments, especially the wording of warrants. It appears that the teacher thought strategically about the various functions and about the sequence in support of the writing of extended definitions. The various structures that the teacher used to prompt and manage discussion influenced the nature of the discussion. While the students took charge of the small-group discussions, the teacher orchestrated the whole process, noting target outcomes, setting time limits, and modeling the process.

Figure 5.1. Percentages of Contributions to Small-Group Survey Discussion

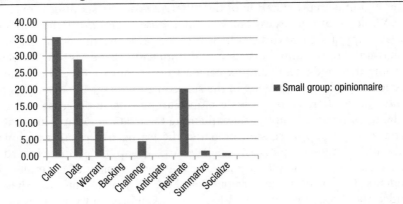

Figure 5.2. Percentages of Contributions to Large-Group Survey Discussion

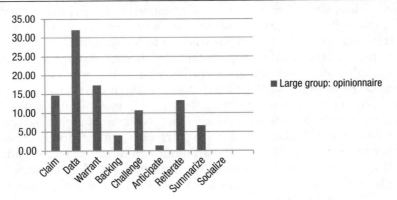

Figure 5.3. Percentages of Contributions to Large-Group Sample Scenario Discussion

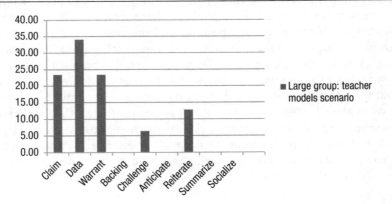

Figure 5.4. Percentages of Contributions to Small-Group Scenario Discussion

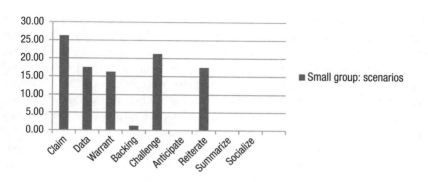

Figure 5.5. Percentages of Contributions to Large-Group Scenario Discussion

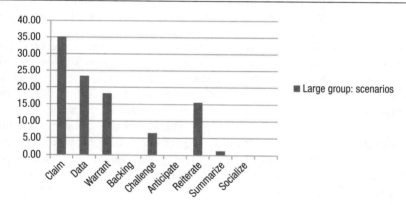

Figure 5.6. Percentages of Contributions to Extended Small-Group Scenario Discussion

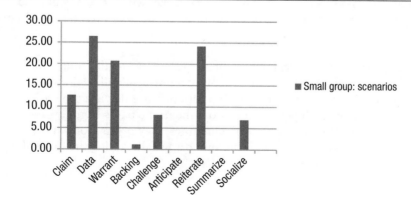

A PURPOSEFUL SEQUENCE OF INQUIRY AND DISCUSSION

Taken as a whole, the sequence of instructional conversations reveals a discussion and inquiry cycle, consisting of at least five phases, if one includes the extension of discussions as the students interact during the planning and composing of their essays and the application of a critical framework (i.e., the criteria for defining the concept of *obligation*) to the analysis of related works of literature. The five phases listed below are part of a broader inquiry process that relies on purposeful peer interaction, writing, and subsequent reading. As the teacher moves the students through the cycle, she monitors what they say, looking for evidence that the students have substantive knowledge, including the procedures for arguing and defining. The teacher's judgments about the learners' proficiency, as displayed during oral discourse, guide her decisions about the pacing of the discussions, the transitioning to a new phase in the sequence, and the possible return to, or review of, an earlier part of the sequence. Any teacher would be wise to follow Ms. Edsel's example in being conscious of the specific function of each discussion (e.g., to support claims with examples, to evaluate competing perspectives) and in looking for evidence that the students were practicing the procedures that the activity was designed to promote. Without relying on a paper-and-pencil assessment, a teacher can hear the evidence that students can or cannot formulate logical arguments and represent fairly and accurately the arguments of others. Three important instructional elements are at work here: (1) the scaffolding of experiences that build on students' knowledge and advance their thinking to greater and greater levels of complexity, (2) the conscious awareness of the specific function of each discussion, and (3) the attention to what learners are saying in order to judge whether they have sufficient command of the procedures that will be important for subsequent tasks and learning.

Taken as a complete cycle, the series of discussions in the observed 9th-grade class followed this function sequence, which extends beyond the preparation for writing and transfers to discussions of literature, and later written responses to the literature:

> *Exploring:* In this exploratory phase, usually in small groups, the
> learners take up the discussion of a problem and begin by
> exploring each participant's position. Since this is a time to
> discover each person's position, the participants begin by asserting
> claims. As the exploration continues, they prompt one another
> to support claims, with the support usually taking the form of
> distilled narratives as examples.

Drafting: Drawing from the earlier small-group discussion, with
the teacher as facilitator, the participants put whole arguments
together, expressing a conclusion supported by an example and
interpreted by citing a general principle. The conversational turns
are longer than in the small-group discussion. As the discussion
progresses, participants challenge one another, with the challenges
usually directed at the warrants.

Synthesizing: As the discussion progresses, with several speakers
expressing fully constructed arguments, the speakers contend
with many arguments, and the process now includes linking,
comparing, and evaluating. The exposure to the body of
arguments invites the participants to make complex judgments
about the central problem.

Applying: The students apply the procedures as they write about the
issue at the heart of the series of discussions. As the students move
away from preparatory activities, they apply the procedures that
they practiced in small-group and large-group discussions to their
judgments about characters in a narrative and about the themes
they derive from their reading.

Extending: Over time, the learners enter into new discussions that
complicate and extend their earlier thinking, usually by asking
them to reconcile discrepancies and to account for new factors.
Students extend their discussions as they read other texts and
begin to connect one to another.

This chapter traced the sequence of discussions in a 9th-grade English
class, as the teacher moved the learners toward writing an academic essay and reading related texts critically. As I emphasized at the beginning of
this chapter, the series of discussions suggest two important considerations
for practice: (1) All discussions are not the same; they do not all serve the
same function; and (2) the nature of the discussions depends on the structures and expectations that the teacher, as the orchestrator for learning,
establishes. The discussions were part of a larger cycle intended to advance
deep understandings and important proficiencies for problem solving, social interaction, and written composition. The pattern has much in common with the idea of "instructional chains" in the teaching of argument
that VanDerHeide and Newell (2013) describe. While Ms. Edsel prepared
students to write an extended definition, the students' composing would
depend on their command of argument. In this case, the teacher moved
students forward in a scaffolded sequence to prepare them to write logically
about an abstract concept.

In the next chapter, I will look at the written product that followed from the sequence of discussions. In interviews, the teacher and her students report their sense of the importance of the discussions to the composing process. I will look also at other classes and other teachers, in both high school (Chapter 7) and a community college (Chapter 8), to confirm that similar discussion sequences exist, with teachers and learners aware of the function of discussion in service of inquiry and writing.

CHAPTER 6

Tracking the Impact of Discussion on Writing

For the purpose of discovering what students do in small group and whole-class discussions that would account for the quality of writing that students produce following their discussion-based preparation, I have looked closely into classrooms in 5th grade, 9th grade, 10th grade, and first-year composition at a community college. I have drawn from several sources of data to identify the practices during discussion that might reveal the many ways in which discussion supports writing: the transcripts of students talking together, the students' writing, students' commentary about their writing, interviews with students, interviews with teachers, and my own classroom observations. I have listed below the obvious benefits that students gained from the discussions I observed and recorded, benefits that are apparent in the transcripts, revealed in the students' writing, and affirmed in the interviews with students and teachers. In the balance of this chapter I illustrate these benefits. In Chapter 8, I return to the summary of benefits of discussion and offer some related recommendations.

WHAT DO STUDENTS GAIN FROM THEIR DISCUSSIONS?

1. Students *learn content*. They test examples as support for claims. They offer examples to account for their judgments about survey items and about assessments of the actions of characters described in scenarios. Students also hear the examples that their classmates cite, offering some models and providing options for supporting their own claims.
2. Students *evaluate examples*. Students evaluate the accuracy of examples and the relevance of examples in supporting claims.
3. Students *scan the variety of opinions* about a question at the heart of the inquiry, revealing that there is doubt and there are competing views. This helps students to represent the field of inquiry and the area of doubt that they need to address in their written response to the problem. This is a necessary element in inquiry.

4. Students *recognize and respond to challenges* to their conclusions, especially about the rules, principles, or warrants they use for interpreting data.
5. Students *practice basic elements of argument* by making claims, citing examples, and interpreting examples.
6. Students *practice uptake*, in that they ground their contributions to discussion by linking them to previous comments.
7. Students *recognize and evaluate competing views*. This is different from observation #4, in that the views may not be in direct opposition to their own—they simply hear and judge the views expressed by others.
8. Students *organize a set of arguments* in a combined analysis to advance a broader purpose (e.g., defining an abstract concept).
9. Students *refine the language* of claims and warrants, especially as a result of their peers' and the teacher's requests for clarity and precision.
10. Students *expand their vocabulary* as they experience language in action.

CONNECTING TALK TO WRITING

In the previous chapter I shared transcripts from small-group and large-group discussions. One of the participants was a student whom I called Kanji. He is one of the students whose classroom talk is represented in the small-group discussion, and he is one of the students whom I interviewed. It is not possible to review several compositions in detail here. Instead, I focus on the writing of one student, whose work the teacher identified as representative of the writing she received from most of the class.

The teacher planned and managed the series of discussions that I presented in Chapter 5 as a substantial part of the students' preparation to write an extended definition about the concept of *obligation*. The definition, which includes the identification of several criteria, was part of a wider inquiry that included the close examination of several texts, including Shel Silverstein's *The Giving Tree*. The writing of the definition preceded the reading of "The Scarlet Ibis" and Steinbeck's *Of Mice and Men*. I have reproduced the teacher's prompt for the writing and Kanji's entire composition here.

WRITING PROMPT: WHAT IS OUR OBLIGATION?

In Charles Dickens's *A Christmas Carol*, a local philanthropist approaches Mr. Scrooge for a donation, saying, "A few of us are endeavouring to raise a fund to buy the Poor some meat and drink, and means of warmth." The man tells Scrooge that many poor people would prefer to die rather than to go to horrible prisons and workhouses, which seem to be their only option for relief. Scrooge responds in this rough way: "If they would rather die, they had better do it, and decrease the surplus population."

Dickens, like many other authors, seems to imply that human beings should feel sympathy and must take some responsibility for the welfare of their fellow human beings, especially for the less fortunate in our communities. At the same time, many thoughtful people who are less callous than Mr. Scrooge will insist that each individual is responsible for his or her own welfare, exercising free choice and assuming personal responsibility so as not to become a burden on others. Many decisions about the role of government and the construction of government budgets rest on the question of our obligation to help fellow human beings.

Since you will be studying some works of literature that explore this conflict, it is important that you establish your own position so that you can read critically. Based on our class discussions and your reaction to hypothetical cases, how would you *define* a human being's *obligation for the welfare of fellow human beings*?

Your *extended* definition should have the following features:

- An introduction in which you show your reader that there is a problem (i.e., when we are obligated to help) to consider and in which you state in summary fashion your position about the problem

- A series of body paragraphs based on the criteria that you and your classmates developed in class

- In each body paragraph, an example that illustrates the criterion statement and is drawn from your own experience, from class discussion, or from your reading and viewing

- In each body paragraph, an explanation of how the example connects with the criterion statement

- A conclusion that reiterates the problem and your general conclusion about the problem

---

STUDENT'S RESPONSE—DO THIS, NOT THAT

KANJI AMAJI

Children nowadays, myself included, are growing up part of the Internet generation; these cohorts are constantly immersed in social media and are utilizing the newest methods for communicating with peers. Long gone are the days of your friends being your neighbors. On Facebook, users consider two hundred, five hundred, upwards of one thousand people to be their "friends." With all of these connections, how do we determine to whom we are truly close or obligated for support? Since we rely on the past to look toward the future, then we have relied on all of those before us to create a better future for us now. Therefore, everyone is to thank for creating the now. So, we should try to help everyone to create a better future for everyone; in essence, we are our brothers' keepers. Therefore, one should fulfill an obligation to all others as long as it doesn't hurt him. However, if one believes it to be important to himself, then he can overlook that previous condition. This is because, as repeatedly shown, sacrifices are made for prized relationships.

Strangers—our brothers—should receive one's goodwill if one believes it to be righteous. In our *Of Mice and Men* pre-reading, we discussed scenario four in-depth. Coach Douglas of Trinity High School considers giving the juvenile delinquents of Gainesville State School some of his team's fans in the upcoming game. Considering that his team is undefeated and will be sure victors in their matchup, offering fans to his opponents will not endanger his team or their spirit; the only imaginable result is that the other will feel uplifted from the support. Given the circumstances, since Coach Douglas and the Trinity Lions will not suffer loss and his idea is morally correct, then he should follow through with his idea. However, sometimes harm can be suffered in the process of helping others. Will Smith stars in the film *Seven Pounds* where he purposefully decides to positively change the lives of seven people. Toward the end, he encounters a man who is blind and a woman with a mortal heart condition whom he decides are worthy for his cause: saving lives. So that doctors can perform cornea and heart transplants to save these two people, he decides to kill himself. Yet, he believed in his decisions to forfeit himself for others. Since it was his moral decision, it was a worthy choice to kill himself for others. He is not in the least obligated to kill himself for them or even recognize their troubles. Deciding to overgo these standards, his conviction in his duty rightly led him to a decision which he therefore felt obligated to fulfill.

From strangers to our strongest devotions, people pay special tribute to affairs that they truly care for: religion and love; since these aspects of life are important, an obligation is felt to obey them. In Islam, there are five pillars of faith which all Muslims must obey to keep their religion. One such pillar, Zakat, is the obligatory charity donation. Yet giving money can be damaging to one's pockets during economic turmoil when times are personally tough. Fortunately for the faithful yet disenfranchised, there are restrictions in ancient texts which state salary requirements to pay and receive the charity. Obligations can be lifted or added so that followers are fair and devoted to their faith. Because there are limits on when charity is applicable, it is guaranteed that Islam's goodwill will not be detrimental to those who pay. From a worldwide religion to an NBC comedy, *Parks and Recreation* shows when one might overcome trouble to display virtuous love. In one episode, Ron—the manliest of men—offers to take care of his girlfriend Diane's grade school daughters. He abhors the task, but he's willing to endure the antics of the girls to show his love for Diane. His obligation to their relationship is considered more important than his personal wants. If one believes in his actions, then he will endure the pain because it is important to him.

Individuals should not forget that they have to consider themselves as well; fulfilling their own needs and wants is also important. In "The Scarlet Ibis," the narrator urges Doodle to progress because it will make the narrator feel better: "I was embarrassed at having a brother of that age who couldn't walk, so I set out to teach him" (page 3). One cannot go through life living a servant to all others. Selfish desires are part of human nature. Doodle is satisfying himself by losing his shame for an invalid brother. Helping Doodle also happens to be a moral side effect. Both of them benefit, so the narrator's execution of a self-obligation is proper. In another piece of literature from this year, Atticus Finch (*To Kill a Mockingbird*) accepted the Tom Robinson case aware, "You might hear some ugly talk about it at school, but do one thing for me if you will: you just hold your head high and keep those fists down" (page 101). Before taking the case, he knew that there would be severe repercussions for him and his family. He has to warn Scout to not react violently now to the criticism for fear of making the situation worse. If he knows that it would bring harm to his family, then why take the case? He truly believed in stepping up for Tom Robinson and his cause. Since he believed in his cause, then the resulting damages can be overlooked.

The more valued a connection is, the more one should be willing to support it. Regardless of the relationship, its value depends on how much one believes. Under these circumstances, a stranger could receive all one has to give, yet a family member could be abused. This simple guideline can lead one to a positive life. In our everyday lives, it may seem trivial to consider such minute analysis to be an important action. For grander determinations where consideration is necessary, it adds an extra level of thought to ensure the correct choice is made in consideration to one and others.

FROM DISCUSSION TO COMPOSITION

Even a cursory review of Kanji's writing reveals transfer from the discussions reported in Chapter 5. First, there are specific references to the discussions. Kanji refers to a claim that "we are our brothers' keepers" (paragraph 1), which was part of the small-group and large-group discussions about the survey about *obligation*. In referring to this adage, he notes that it is conditional, identifying the area of doubt at the center of the discussions: "Therefore, one should fulfill an obligation to all others as long as it doesn't hurt him. However, if one believes it to be important to himself, then he can overlook that previous condition." An element of Kanji's introduction is the framing of a problem—that the adage generally applies, but one's obligation depends on the nature of the relationship with a fellow human (i.e., one's "brother") and the risk to oneself.

In the second paragraph, Kanji notes specifically that "we discussed scenario four in-depth." He assumes that the reader is familiar with the scenario and the discussion, recognizing the reality that the teacher is the primary reader. He refers to the details of the scenario and adds to it with another example from a Will Smith movie to qualify his conclusion and to complicate the criterion that one is obligated to help others if "one believes it to be righteous." Kanji is consistent in offering examples to support his assertions. Certainly throughout the discussion Kanji practiced this procedure of citing data to support claims. It is reasonable to expect that the series of discussions, involving prompts and questions from the teacher and peers, helped Kanji as a writer to anticipate that readers might question his claims and expect support for his generalizations. The discussions also seem to have revealed to Kanji that there are nuances to the rules that a group might devise to guide behavior, so he looks beyond the scenario discussed in class to add another level of complexity to show that circumstances might invite one to reassess the rule.

Part of writing an extended definition of an abstract concept is the identifying of criteria that suggest the limits of the concept and distinguish it from other, similar concepts. In this case, Kanji builds on the criteria that the class derived through their series of discussions. He draws on examples from the scenarios, from the instances that his classmates described, and from his own reflection. He refers to a specific scenario, but he also refers to discussions of related literature from the current line of inquiry and from an earlier unit of study during the school year.

At one stage in the process of facilitating the students' compositions of the definitions, Ms. Edsel asked the students to print a version triple-spaced with wide margins. She directed the students to review their compositions, paragraph by paragraph, and write in the margins their answers to this question: How did you know this in order to write this part of your composition? In his introduction, Kanji refers to the superficial conception of *friends* as the term is used in the world of social media. He comments on the meaning of his reference: "Ms. Edsel taught us to ask ourselves 'So what?'/'What does it mean?'" It appears that he hears a critical voice, like those he has heard in many discussions, asking for an explanation of the significance of the Facebook example. Referring to the same paragraph, Kanji cites classroom discussion specifically as a source of knowledge for his writing: "We held a discussion about 'brother's keepers' in class, which led me to believe its truth. We also discussed, and I agreed, that if it doesn't hurt one, then they should do it."

Referring to the second paragraph, he notes that the criterion statement that he offers derives from class discussion: "I initially thought—to general consensus—that Coach should help in scenario four. I knew it was a legitimate, common belief/conclusion." He also notes that while the classroom discussions offered much, he added his own reflection in order to extend the thinking evident in the discussions. Citing the example from a Will Smith movie, Kanji recalls, "I took an entire day to think about sources outside of discussions for this paper. My thinking of sacrifice led me to a movie which I had watched before."

Kanji also drew from discussions about literature. First, he cites from the short story "The Scarlet Ibis," noting in his margin comment that the citation is a "powerful, highly discussed, quote from "Scarlet Ibis" in class." He notes that earlier discussions about *To Kill a Mockingbird* influenced his reference to Atticus Finch as an example. He also notes the effect of earlier discussions about *Romeo and Juliet* to help him to qualify claims about obligation to others: "During our Romeo and Juliet unit, I thought for our final paper we discussed relationships: importance of many relationships."

STUDENTS' REFLECTIONS ON THEIR OWN WRITING

After the students had written their essays, I had an opportunity to interview the students whose small-group discussions I had recorded. The interview questions appear as Appendix E. Six of the eleven students I interviewed cited classroom discussions as a key element in helping them to write an elaborated composition. I begin with some responses from Kanji and then share similar observations from other students.

McCann: So, when you have to write a composition for school, what helps you? What enables you to do that?

Kanji: Um . . . I'd say I get ideas from what we talk about in class, and the . . . Talking with classmates, like, in class and outside of class to get ideas, but also, during the assignments, I try to keep it in my mind so I can point it out whenever I see a connection between the assignment and what I'm doing in life.

McCann: If you think about this one fairly long composition, what helped you with this one, particularly?

Kanji: Uh, I think the materials that we received in class, and then explaining them separately and together to see how the teacher wants the material written, and what kind of material she wants included.

McCann: Can you tell me about how the materials . . . what kind of materials are you referring to, and how they might help you?

Kanji: Um . . . so that would be the evidence that we used for, to prove our claim in class. Um. So, just . . . for instance, for this most recent essay, we had to . . . we read *The Giving Tree,* and, just seeing how it can . . . not necessarily be *anything* related, but it does, it does, it doesn't have to be a long novel. It can be a children's story. It can be a TV show. Whatever. It's . . . you have a variety of sources to choose from.

In the interview, Kanji notes that his talking with classmates, in class and outside of class, helps him generally in writing compositions in school and helped especially with the most recent writing. He refers to the importance of the materials that the teacher provides. The materials, including Silverstein's *The Giving Tree*, introduced problems with which the students grappled together in small groups and as a whole class. He notes that it is important to be aware of the teacher's expectations, but these expectations align with the class' expression of a quality standard for good writing in general. Kanji seems to have learned the language of argument—expressing claims, citing data, applying warrants to interpret data—from the teacher's modeling and from the class discussions. While an extended definition might be categorized as exposition, such a composition relies on argument, in which the units of thought include claims supported by relevant data, interpreted by citing the aligned warrants.

The following exchange with a student I call Mike reveals his understanding of the importance of discussion, both in the classroom and beyond, even with reliance on social media as the vehicle for having the discussion. Although Kanji emphasizes the value of discussion as part of the preparation for writing, Mike notes that he benefits from talking to peers throughout the writing process, including an editing stage, "because you can get more than one opinion."

McCann: OK. When you write a composition for school, what helps you?
Mike: I usually . . . a lot of student help. I ask the other students, and they ask me, and we all share ideas, kind of. And having other people edit your essays is always helpful, because you can get more than one opinion.
McCann: Um, tell me about this process of sharing ideas. How does . . . how does that occur?
Mike: Well, sometimes students will just, like . . . we'll talk about evidence we used, or, like, just general ideas of, like, how we're writing or what we're writing. Like, what your stance on the essay prompt is.
McCann: Does this occur informally outside of class, or is it something you do as part of the teacher's plan in class?
Mike: It's usually just on Facebook. We just ask each other. It's not really, like, getting a lot. It's just general ideas.

The interactions among peers help the students to develop knowledge about the substance at the center of their inquiry, and about the procedures for making critical judgments and advancing their own arguments in the face of competing arguments. These benefits for learning how to write elaborated and logical compositions are evident from these sources: students' interactions in classroom discussion, as reported in Chapter 5; the subsequent writing they produce, as represented by Kanji's composition; and their reflections on the processes they follow during discussions and in composing their essays. Teachers also testified to the many ways that discussion supports writing. In the balance of this chapter and in Chapter 8, you will hear from teachers from high school to college as they describe their inquiry-based approaches to teaching students to write well and note the function of discussions in the learning process. I draw these testimonials from interviews with the teachers. The interview questions appear as Appendix F.

TEACHERS' REFLECTIONS ON DISCUSSION AND WRITING

Ms. Edsel, the teacher whose students feature prominently in Chapter 5, reports many of the complexities involved in planning, managing, facilitating, monitoring, and refining writing instruction. She describes a planning approach that relies on her knowing her students well. The scaffolding she describes includes her tapping into students' funds of knowledge about argument and about the substantive issues at the heart of their discussions. She values students' collaboration, and she tracks their discussions to reveal to her whether students exhibit the habits of thinking that align with the kind of writing for which they are preparing. Perhaps most important, Ms. Edsel appreciates that students cannot write much of substance unless they have thought thoroughly about the concepts and complexities at the heart of the problem they are discussing. As Ms. Edsel has demonstrated in her instructional sequence, the series of connected discussions immerse students in the procedures for argument, definition, and critical judgment, and expose them to content related to the current inquiry, including a variety of examples and competing analyses.

If the patterns of classroom discourse reported by Nystrand (1997) continued to apply today, Ms. Edsel would be the rare teacher who regularly engages students in *authentic discussion*, distinct from *recitation*, in that the classroom conversations focus on problems and questions that do not have prespecified answers. Rarer still, Ms. Edsel plans the conversations so that they build on what students already know, build in a sequence that attends to instructional needs and the developing complexity of the problem, and involve the students in the procedures that will be necessary for composing an elaborated essay. Here Ms. Edsel speaks about her instructional intentions:

I think students learn collaboratively, and so I think that that would be one of the, one of the things that help, I think, in writing instruction, that kids . . . that kids have . . . . You know, they've been writing, before they come to me, they've been writing for a long time, and they do have some knowledge about, um, what they've been teaching, what they've been taught, or they've had experiences writing, you know, whether it be, like, academic, or writing a letter. And so, I think, one thing would be that students have some knowledge about what writing is, or what they believe writing is. And so part of it is working with, like, where students are in terms of writing, and figuring out where they are, and then designing instruction to meet them where they are and take them where they need to go.

For Ms. Edsel, the classroom interactions allow her to infer what students already know and help her to judge students' progress toward the instructional targets related to writing an extended definition and reading complex texts critically. She relies on students' informal writing to see progress, but she also can assess development by attending to contributions during discussions: "I'm also doing that in their discussion, or, like, when we're reading. So I'm also, even if they're not writing the evidence down, if they have to kind of defend a position in a class discussion, and they're choosing evidence, I know, hey, they can do this in the speaking; what's the issue in the writing that . . . what's the connection that I need to make?"

For Ms. Edsel, teaching students to write extended definitions or other academic essays that build on argument requires more than exposing students to a template or organizational framework; students need to have a deep understanding of the substance about which they are writing:

You know, writing is as much of, I think, of form as *content*. So, it's not only about kids creating a framework for argument, you know, using the framework of argument. It's also, what's the content of this essay going to be? So, for instance, if kids are writing a definition of *obligation* paper, like, you know, for this study, or, um, you know, to what extent should I protect the innocent from the evil of the world, which is one of my questions for *The Catcher in the Rye*, kids have to know that. Like, what does it mean to be innocent? What does it mean . . . what does *obligation* mean? And if they can't negotiate those higher principles, while they might have what looks like a paper, a framework of argument, the framework, the content of the paper, also, could be lacking if they don't understand the different ways you can define *innocence*. So I think it's as much of allowing kids to have these discussions about what the content of the posttest . . . you know, the unit from the pretest to the posttest is so they're not only, like, they're not only practicing the skills, but they're negotiating the ideas collectively together, and defining them and redefining them, and applying them in various situations.

This teacher's testimonial suggests that if writing arguments or definitions were only a matter of familiarity with an organizational or rhetorical structure, then the writers could insert almost any content to make the composition work. But for Ms. Edsel, if students are to write anything that is honest and significant—in the sense of addressing real problems in a thorough, accurate, and logical way—then the series of discussions that precede the writing must involve students in the argument moves or procedures and help them to find, evaluate, and organize the kind of criteria and examples that will be the substance of their writing.

Ms. Edsel sees the discussions that precede the writing of an extended definition and the composition itself as part of a larger course of inquiry that binds the many literacy experiences of her class together and invests her students in the activities of the class. She has observed the complexity of the discussions of her class:

> And so I think those discussions allow students not only the opportunity to take risks with the framework of argumentation, and so forth, but also allows them to think, to kind of develop a more complete and thorough interpretation, which not only proves what they think of their opinion, but considers how the opposition might respond, which, oftentimes I think that kids forget that, um, that writing is, maybe, a large . . . just part of a larger conversation, so writers often predict what other people think or how other people might interpret this, and incorporate that. So, I think the discussions allow, allow students to have a more thorough understanding of the content.

Ms. Edsel also recognizes the function of discussions, especially in small groups, in supporting the sense of community among learners. She judges that students still complete most academic writing because it is an assigned task: "I think you have to engage them. Like, you have to give them, writing purpose. And too often, writing . . . there's no purpose in writing. Kids just see it as, you know, I'm going to tell the teacher what they need to know. I'm going to, um, get this done." In contrast, Ms. Edsel intends to invite students into inquiry processes that involve substantive discussion about problems that resonate with them. Through the teacher's modeling and through a sequence of discussions, the students learn procedures for argument and definition, and they apply the procedures in thinking about significant issues. Ms. Edsel continues:

> It's when they have to actually utilize those to, like, solve larger problems. That's where the, that's where the engagement is going to occur, and that's where it's going to get kids revved up to walk into class, because even though they're using this framework of argument for writing, it's really seeing how effectively they can use it; can they change other people's minds using it? And then having these larger issues, like, you know, "What is evil in the world?" Kids want to . . . kids are trying to figure that out on their own. Or, "to whom or what do I remain loyal?" All kids are struggling with declaring loyalty and the consequences or benefits of doing so. And so, I think once they see how, um . . . I mean, that's the positive experience, I think, when students start to see that these skills are not skills that are limited to the classroom or to English or even to academia, but they're skills that they're going to have to use as they try to convince their parents, you know, for an extended curfew. But these skills have, if you're a thinking person, they're what you use to solve problems.

The practices of 5th-grade teachers Ms. Boski and Ms. Wieczorek, as reported in Chapters 3 and 4, and the experiences in Ms. Edsel's class, as reported in this chapter and Chapter 5, are probably not common among teachers of writing. But teachers in other contexts, working with students at various developmental levels, also follow an inquiry and dialogic path to helping students to write logical and elaborated compositions. I have observed similar patterns and similar sequences of discussion in a 10th-grade classroom (Chapters 2 and 7), and in a first-year composition course at a community college (see Chapter 8). In short, the teachers operate strategically, not thinking of each discussion as an isolated experience, but planning each discussion as part of a connected sequence, with each discussion building on a previous one and preparing learners for subsequent discussions. Each discussion is part of a larger inquiry process. The teacher has in mind a specific purpose for each discussion (e.g., to generate criteria, to identify and evaluate examples, etc.) and monitors the conversation to judge the extent to which the discussion advances the purpose. The observed teachers check regularly that the talk among peers prepares learners for subsequent writing and for developing the procedures for advancing the inquiry across several texts and conversations.

CHAPTER 7

Some Assembly Required: Building Inquiry-Based Learning Activities

QUESTIONS AND PROBLEMS

Inquiry and discussion do not just happen. The teachers featured in this book all report that they made careful plans to initiate inquiry and to prompt and sustain discussion. Perhaps some teachers can enter a classroom and, without a great deal of planning, pose a question that draws all students into a lively discussion and course of inquiry. But teachers whose work I examine in this book have found it useful to introduce students to a specific problem that invests the learners in collaborative work, research, extended discussion, and elaborated writing. The problem typically takes the form of a narrative, such as a scenario, case study, or simulation, with specific characters, a recognizable conflict, and sufficient detail to complicate matters and to support deliberation. This chapter suggests sources for such problems and walks the reader through the process of constructing an inquiry-based instructional activity. Of course, instruction that helps students to think critically and to write elaborated academic essays is not simply a matter of distributing printed cases and directing students to solve problems. The teacher still has to orchestrate learning and facilitate authentic discussions. This chapter also traces the patterns of practice among teachers who assume an inquiry stance and skillfully facilitate discussions.

Every morning when I open up my newspaper, problems jump out at me. Some of the problems are complex and technical (e.g., the potential for regulating financial institutions engaged in exotic derivatives trading) or are far removed from the experiences of most teenagers and other young learners (e.g., Tibetans seeking independence from China); but other problems strike me as resonant with adolescents. Perhaps the news story describes issues about fairness and justice, about young romance thwarted by narrow-minded adults, about challenges to friendship, or about the tension between demands for allegiance to authority and the need for independence. It is probably my decades of classroom experience that influence my attention to such stories. Although it is never an absolute certainty that a story that I find compelling also will be compelling to students, it is possible to make reasonable guesses about the kind of stories that spark interest and trigger a course of inquiry, as I suggest in Chapter 2.

As Wiggins and McTighe (2005) and Burke (2010) propose, relying on essential questions can imbue literacy activities with meaning and significance, can prompt inquiry, and can provide the bond that connects reading, writing, speaking, and listening experiences into a coherent whole. But, as I note in Chapter 2, the essential questions by themselves can remain vaguely abstract and obscurely remote for many students. What, after all, makes an "essential question" *essential*? I judge that adolescents and other younger learners appreciate the narratives that raise or suggest compelling questions that can be essential to a discipline. The narratives attached to news stories, history, imaginative literature, and films present learners with very specific problems, with apparent conflicts, real human participants, and intriguing complications. My experience tells me that it is the tangible problem that raises questions, initiates inquiry, and spurs discussions that lead to the reading of complex texts and to the writing of elaborated compositions.

Sometimes a news story or other narrative by itself will spark students' inquiry. But often news stories betray a biased view of matters, and this bias compromises genuine inquiry. Often curious readers also can trace news stories to their culmination; for example, a court decision, a settlement, or a subsequent discovery, all of which eliminate the doubt that drives the inquiry. At other times the narratives drawn from imaginative literature require an introduction that activates prior knowledge and that engages students in the critical thinking that tough issues and complex texts require. Several sources provide examples of rich inquiry-based activities that invite critical thinking and prompt extensive discussions and elaborated writing. Appendix G lists some of these sources. A teacher could tap such sources to develop an extensive repertoire of ways to initiate inquiry, but there might be occasions when the teacher needs to construct an inquiry activity that will engage a specific group of learners and invite a connected sequence of discussions, readings, and extensive writing. The following guide suggests a process for developing one kind of inquiry activity, a case study drawn from news reports and appropriate for developing into a simulation role-playing activity.

Of course, the activity does not facilitate itself. It is possible for a teacher using a problem-based activity to dominate discussion, take control of the analysis of the problem, and reduce the case to simple recall and recitation. After offering a guide to constructing an inquiry-based learning activity and drawing from the examples of the teachers profiled in earlier chapters, I describe also the "moves" that a teacher would likely make in introducing a problem; managing small-group work; monitoring group progress; facilitating large-group discussion; assessing the proficiencies that the activities are intended to promote; summarizing deliberations, consensus, and continuing doubt; and transitioning to the subsequent reading, writing, and other extensions to the initial inquiry.

GUIDE TO CONSTRUCTING INQUIRY-BASED ACTIVITIES

Of course, the construction of an instructional activity will depend on an awareness of specific learning targets and on the teacher's deep knowledge of the specific learners. In Chapter 3, the 5th-grade teachers' work illustrates this attempt to align goals, characteristics of the learners, and instructional activities. Smagorinsky (2007) describes this alignment in detail in his guide to designing instructional units. With an awareness of learning targets and attention to the needs and interests of specific learners, a teacher can troll various sources to discover the problems that are likely to attract students and trigger an inquiry process. It is useful to also consult Troyka (1974) to see models for simulation role-playing activities, Gee (2007) to learn a "design grammar" for the kind of video games that engross users, and Newmann et al. (1996) for criteria for instructional activities that have intellectual merit. The following descriptions trace the process of transforming a news story into a problem-based instructional activity.

A news story in the *New York Times* reported that a school closure in Philadelphia would require that students from one high school soon be absorbed into another school (Logman, 2013). This unwelcome closure of a school and its merger into another is a recurring problem (see, e.g., Hu, 2007; Ahmed-Ullah, Chase, & Secter, 2013). Such a change would be traumatic enough for many students and their parents; but in the Philadelphia case, the schools had long been archrivals in interscholastic athletics. For many of the athletes from the closing school, it would be distasteful, if not impossible, to join as a teammate with the formerly hated rivals, even when the transferring student athlete had a passion for a sport. This combination of fears, loyalties, potential friendship, potential rejection, identity challenge, and loss makes the case a likely candidate to grabs learners' interests and set them on a course of inquiry. The case might serve as an appropriate invitation to students to think about issues related to *loyalty, values,* and *identity* that are at the core of a broader inquiry in an conceptual unit that includes attention to a variety of texts that treat these issues in complex ways. But the case as reported in the news focuses on the insensitivity of a school board and the resiliency of coaches and athletes; and by the time students in other classrooms see the case, matters will be settled. To prompt inquiry, the doubt must remain; and to follow through with the inquiry, students must have access to information and have opportunities to deliberate and debate in the appropriate forums. To transform the news story, then, into a problem-based case, a teacher would need to attend to the criteria described in Chapter 2. It is key that the fictionalized version of the story emphasize that there is a problem that still requires investigation, and that the investigation benefits from purposeful interactions among peers. Also, a written response to the case will be the logical product of the deliberation. Again, it will be helpful to offer students a prompt that recalls the central problem, recognizes its complexity, and suggests an audience and a standard for addressing the audience.

A SAMPLE CASE

Here, then, is a sample problem-based case that engaged a group of 10th-graders as part of a conceptual unit that focused on the concept of *loyalty*. The case appears below, followed by sample portions of discussion among the 10th-graders. I comment on the features of the discussion, suggesting the elements of the case that promoted inquiry and discussion. I also highlight one 10th-grade teacher to underscore the elements of his practice that foster and sustain inquiry and discussion.

Loyal to You, Gresham High

The school year began with rumors that Walter Quintin Gresham High School, home of the Monarchs, would close for good at the end of the current school year. A series of contentious meetings of the City Schools Board of Education and several neighborhood protests could not hold back the inevitable. The enrollment had been dwindling for years, and Gresham, which had opened in 1871, was in sorry disrepair and had become too expensive to renovate. The current graduating class would be the last one, and the remaining students would move next year to Oakdale High School, home of the Hornets, a little over 2 miles away. At graduation, students, parents, teachers, and alumni sang together for the last time the Gresham spirit song, modeled after the school song from the University of Illinois:

We're loyal to you, Gresham High!
We're true royal blue, Gresham High!
We'll all take a stand against the best in the land,
'Cause you have our hands, Gresham High!

A DIFFICULT TRANSITION

Students and their parents imagined that it was going to be difficult to transition to a new school in the coming year. A change to an unfamiliar school in a different neighborhood would be daunting for almost any adolescent, but the situation at Gresham would be particularly stressful. Beyond facing the new transportation challenges to a school that would no longer be the "neighborhood school," students would have to find their way around a different building, learn new routines, and familiarize themselves with new teachers, counselors, and deans. But there would be more significant challenges. The student body at Gresham had been predominantly Mexican American, and the school celebrated Mexican heritage in many ways. One long wall in the cafeteria displayed a colorful mural that depicted significant moments in Mexican history. The school had a Mexican dance troupe. The library held an extensive collection of literature by Mexican writers. The school sponsored visits by Mexican and Mexican American poets, dancers, musicians, and visual artists. While there would be a significant Latino population at Oakdale, the student body was a diverse mix of ethnicities, including students from families from eastern European countries and more recent immigrants from Vietnam, India, and Palestine.

Certainly the diversity of the reconstituted student body at Oakdale would be something to celebrate, but there was the realistic fear of conflict between the small portions of the student body from each school that were affiliated with street gangs. The dominant gang from the Gresham neighborhood was the J Street Royals, whose representative color was royal blue, the same as in the royal blue and white school colors of Gresham High. At Oakdale, the one obvious gang was the Stingers, represented by black and gold, also the school colors of the high school. Parents and students realized that it would be seriously dangerous for the transferring Gresham students to wear their old school spirit wear to Oakdale, taking great risks to be walking through the neighborhood or riding a bus while flaunting royal blue.

For many of the former Gresham High students, the move to Oakdale would be a difficult one. But the change would be most difficult perhaps for the athletes, especially those who wished to participate in fall sports—football, boys' soccer, and girls' volleyball.

FOR YOUR CONSIDERATION: WHAT SHOULD THE ATHLETES FROM GRESHAM HIGH SCHOOL DO ABOUT JOINING FALL SPORTS AT OAKDALE HIGH? WHAT CAN ADULTS DO TO MAKE THE TRANSITION AS SAFE AND EASY AS POSSIBLE?

Discuss this problem with three or four of your classmates. Your group should focus initially on one perspective so that you can help your classmates to view the problem from this perspective. See the perspectives listed below. Then you will join all of your classmates in seeking a solution to the problem that the athletes face.

With your partners, prepare an argument for addressing the problem. Your argument should attend to the following basic issues:

- Who could be harmed when the former Gresham athletes join, or attempt to join, the fall sports teams at Oakdale? Realistically, how significant are these harms?

- How could the former Gresham athletes be harmed if they choose *not* to join fall sports teams at Oakdale? Realistically, how significant are these harms? In other words, how important is it that the athletes who wish to play on the Oakdale teams can continue to have a positive experience in sports?

- Is there anything that coaches and athletes from both schools can do to make the transition easier? Is there anything that teachers and counselors can do? Describe what this plan would be. What would be the benefits? Can the plan cause any additional problems?

- Can you think of an alternative that would help the former Gresham students to avoid the kind of distress that they anticipate? What would this alternative be? How do you know it would be both a viable (workable) and beneficial alternative?

Perspectives on the Merger

Athletes from Gresham: As you can imagine, the athletes from Gresham worry about the loss of their identity as Gresham Monarchs. They also will find it distasteful, to say the least, to wear the Oakdale colors. The rivalry between the two schools has been bitter, with some meetings ending in fights among the fans. Wearing the colors of their rivals will make the students from Gresham feel that they are betraying their former teammates and all their fellow students from Gresham. Beyond experiencing a sense of betrayal, the Gresham athletes consider the real fear of attack when they wear the colors associated with a street gang from the next neighborhood. The Gresham athletes also worry about rejection. They suspect that their new coaches will be prejudiced against them, perhaps cutting them from teams or relegating them to back-up roles on the squads. While thinking about this perspective, you might want to research articles about athletes who have faced similar situations.

Athletes from Oakdale: As you can imagine, the Oakdale athletes have some mixed feelings about bringing the athletes from Gresham onto their teams. In some cases, the merger is likely to strengthen the team. For example, in the past 10 years the Gresham boys' soccer team has been strong, even winning two regional championships. The addition of these soccer players will only strengthen the team. But the Gresham football team and the girls' volleyball team have been the conference doormats for a long time. The transfer of these athletes to Oakdale will not heighten competition, but could breed conflict and resentment if many of the Gresham players are cut or have to serve as back-ups. For any team to perform at a high level, there must be a feeling of solidarity, which will be difficult to achieve. While thinking about this perspective, you might want to research articles about student athletes who have faced similar circumstances.

Coaches from both schools: Some coaches from Gresham anticipate that the Oakdale coaches will reject their players or not treat them fairly, although they hesitate to express this claim openly. In some instances, the coaches would rather their former athletes not play at all, rather than contribute to the success of Oakdale. From the point of view of the Gresham coaches, the Oakdale coaches and athletes have always had the advantage of better equipment, better facilities, and a larger talent pool. For their part, the Oakdale coaches see potential both for an infusion of talent and for conflict. Some of the Oakdale coaches have criticized the Gresham players for lacking discipline and commitment. The addition of such players would hardly help their teams. While thinking about this perspective, you might want to research articles about coaches who have faced similar circumstances.

Neighborhood teens: Many teens from the Gresham area harbor a deep-seated hatred for Oakdale. Some of them have even sworn that they will drop out of school altogether rather than attend Oakdale. In a sense, the move would mean turning their backs on traditions, on familiar territory, and on sense of pride. They have been "proud to be Monarchs," and would "hate to be Hornets." They would rather the former Gresham athletes transfer to private or parochial schools or not join teams at all, rather than lose their identity in being absorbed into the Oakdale sports culture. Some teens associate themselves one way or another with the J Street Royals gang, and they judge that they would risk their lives by wearing the Hornets colors, which are also associated with the Stingers, a rival gang. In their protests over the past year, many parents have expressed fear for their children's safety. The student athletes would be especially vulnerable, because they might be wearing team colors as they travel home long after most other students and school personnel are gone. While thinking about this perspective, you might want to research articles about high school students who have faced similar circumstances.

Parents from Gresham: Many of the parents of athletes from Gresham have a realistic fear for the students' safety, including the possible emotional damage from rejection and feelings of inferiority. Perhaps less realistically, many parents see their children's success in athletic competition as the only faint possibility that the students will be able to afford college. The most accomplished athletes could earn scholarships worth tens of thousands of dollars. Many Gresham parents, some who endure poverty and some who earn modest incomes, judge that they would never be able to afford college tuition. At the same time, they cannot afford to send their children to private or parochial schools. Some of the parochial schools in the city would accept the student athletes from Gresham, but the tuition at these schools would be equivalent to paying tuition at an in-state public university. The parents would like some assurance that their children will be safe and that they will have a fair opportunity to compete for places on the teams. Although the parents understand the students' fears, they are willing to accept that their children might endure some hardships in the near term in order to have a chance at greater rewards in the future. While thinking about this perspective, you might want to research articles about athletic scholarships and earning potential for college graduates. You also might look into protests in cities where the school board has closed schools.

Teachers, Counselors, and Deans: When the Gresham students transfer to Oakdale, some faculty members also will move to this new environment, including counselors and one dean. The faculty members all want to work in a supportive learning environment, where all students feel safe and valued. The counselors and deans in particular are committed to being proactive in resolving conflict and keeping the school peaceful. The counselors and deans hope to use "advisory periods" to have faculty members model for students how to work through conflict in a constructive way. Of course, there is no guarantee that conflict can be avoided; perhaps some harm to students can be expected when the two rival schools merge. A couple of teachers transferring from Gresham have pledged to begin a Mexican Heritage Club at Oakdale, if there are sufficient funds to support it. While thinking about this perspective, you might want to research articles about teachers and counselors who have faced similar circumstances.

Reading Related to the Case: You might find it useful to read about similar cases in various school systems. The news reports reveal how a school might help to define a neighborhood, how students might be at risk as they venture from their home neighborhood to another, and how the historical rivalries between schools make it difficult to merge. Articles such as the following do not deliver solutions to the problem, but they reveal what people experience and how they respond to the stress of a merger with a rival school:

Jere Logman, "An Involuntary Union of Football Rivals for Philadelphia High Schools." *New York Times,* August 3, 2013.

Winnie Hu, "After 88 Years of Rivalry, the Last as Us and Them." *New York Times,* November 22, 2007.

Noreen S. Ahmed-Ullah, John Chase, and Bob Secter. "CPS Approves Largest School Closure in Chicago's History," *Chicago Tribune,* May 23, 2013.

WORKING WITH THE CASE

On its surface, the Gresham High case would seem to be the kind of inquiry-based activity that would spark discussion and engage adolescent learners in the procedures that are important to the deliberations and critical thinking that lead to elaborated and logical writing. The activity also appears to have the potential to prepare learners for reading and connecting complex texts. In judging the quality of the case as an instructional activity, one might say that it has "face validity," in that it *appears* on first examination to be able to foster the kind of learning about writing arguments that a teacher might hope for. In addition, the case prompts activity, especially discussions in small groups and a large group, reading about related cases to expand thinking and support claims, and the subsequent writing. The case as it is structured seems likely to support the kind of "authentic pedagogy" that has intellectual merit, as envisioned by Newmann et al. (1996). First, as the students contribute to the discussions, listen to one another, contend with challenges and exceptions, add new considerations, read about related situations, draft notes, and attempt and refine an essay, they construct knowledge about a critical problem and its possible solutions. The discussion and writing are part of what Newmann et al. call "disciplined inquiry" (p. 283) in that the learners tap their own funds of knowledge about loyalty, identity, and conflicts; construct a deep understanding about concepts through the give-and-take of deliberation and debate; and communicate their findings and understandings in complex ways through oral discourse and written response.

It is possible, however, for a teacher to transform something that seems like inquiry and offers the potential for authentic pedagogy so that instruction and learning become a monologic affair, with the teacher commanding most of the analysis and the learners trying to recall what the teacher said. I report below some of the key moves of 10th-grade teacher Mr. Minton as he initiates the inquiry, fosters purposeful discussions, and transitions into writing about the case and connecting the discussions to the examination of literature. Drawing from an interview with Mr. Minton, I reveal his conscious decision making during the instructional sequence. Mr. Minton's pedagogical moves are consistent with the practices that Nystrand (1997) and his colleagues associate with "authentic discussion," and they align with the practices that my colleagues and I promote in a book about discussion (McCann, Johannessen, Kahn, & Flanagan, 2006). Juzwik et al. (2013) describe a variety of structures and forums to promote discussion that offer several alternatives to the processes presented below.

DISCUSSING THE CASE

Mr. Minton provided a handout that offered directions for the discussions. He had predetermined the make-up of each group and listed the groups on the board. He indicated where each group should meet. Mr. Minton then directed the small-group work in this way:

> Now that you have read the case, we will spend some time in groups
> to imagine the various perspectives about what to do in this situation.

Here are the core questions: What should the transferring Gresham students, especially the athletes, do in response to the directive to move from their familiar school to one that they don't particularly like? What can students, parents, coaches, and teachers do to ease the transition from one school to another? To appreciate how hard the situation is and the potential to encourage positive outcomes, you will talk in your groups about what various affected people would have to say. So, keep those two core questions in mind and look at the questions on the handout. You have the next 15 minutes to discuss in your groups, and then anyone in your group should be able to report to the rest of us what the assigned students, parents, coaches, or faculty members would have to say.

In one group, a student began the conversation by reading a portion of the case narrative aloud. She highlighted sections of the text as she proceeded. Then the students reacted.

Dana: What's the question then? We are Oakdale. What do we think?

Carly: Wait. Write the question first.

Dana: What would the Oakdale athletes say?

Shaun: I would think that we would take the good players to make our team better.

Carly: You would want the players who have skills and knowledge of the game. That can only make our team better. They shouldn't be discriminated against.

Dana: We are closely looking at the way . . .

Carly: . . . the skills of the athletes.

Dana: Inviting. Inviting. We should invite them. The skills of the players and their knowledge of the sport should secure them a space, a higher space, on the team.

Shaun: By adding good players to the team, we are going to benefit.

Dana: We want them to try out.

Shaun: It is like if Prairie Shores (student's home school) and Lake Plains (a rival school) merged. Lake Plains has a really solid football team. Why wouldn't we want them to be on the team? When athletes are on a team, they get really close together. It doesn't matter where they are from. They become friends.

Carly: We could use this (reads): "solidarity of the team," united.

Dana: I don't think there would be that much anxiety.

Kassie: If the players wear the colors of the old team, they could be harmed because they are gang colors.

Carly: At Gresham High they celebrated Latino culture. So if they do that at Oakdale, . . .

Shaun: The combined teams will be stronger.

Kassie: They could re-make the high school.

Dana: They could change to new colors.

Carly: What if they come to our school?

Dana: They don't like it.

Carly: Gresham has been successful at soccer (reads from the text).

Kassie (referring to the text of the case): The rivalry has been bitter. The former Gresham athletes will feel they are betraying . . .

This discussion and similar small-group conversations continued along these lines, with students trying to imagine what a person in the case would be feeling. They sorted out what they were supposed to be imagining and they projected the complexities of the situation, considering the various benefits possible (e.g., college scholarships) and the potential negatives (from distasteful wearing of opposing colors to the possible attack from neighborhood gangs) associated with choices. As the students explored the position, they prepared to represent this point of view in the whole-class discussion, just as other students in other groups were doing.

Mr. Minton moved around the room, positioning himself to pay close attention to one group at a time, while monitoring the work across the whole class. When he was satisfied that students had sufficiently developed the arguments representing the various points of view, he called all of the students together into a larger forum to share the results of their small-group explorations. Here is how Mr. Minton initiated the large-group discussion:

Mr. Minton: Realize that our thinking today is part of a larger look at our sense of the importance of *loyalty*, or our sense of what it means to be loyal. In the reading that we do in the coming weeks, various characters are caught in conflicts related to their sense of loyalty and the demands on them to be loyal. Remember that for now, you will be writing about this case, so you will want to take some notes about what other people say. OK, then, let's start with some of the coaches from Oakdale.

Larry: I'm a coach. I believe that the team rivalry shows that there should be two teams to maintain peace. Many students from Gresham and Oakdale have a rivalry. It's shown that mixing the athletes might cause violence.

Sarah: I disagree, because we would be promoting disunity.

Kevin (Gresham athlete): I don't want to be associated with the Oakdale athletes at all. I hate them.

Greg (neighborhood teen): I think that you shouldn't have anything to do with them, and not wear their colors.

Sarah: If we do unite them, we might promote to other schools that we don't care about friendship and peace, but the success of the team.

Shaun: We are just strengthening our team to have the best chance to win.

Olivia (as a Gresham parent): I am worried about the potential for violence. I see that the two separate teams will keep the violence down.

Riley (as a Gresham coach): If we are going to have separate teams, isn't it better to promote the safety of the members of the teams?

Kevin: If we do join with Oakdale, the coaches will not give us as much playing time and fairness.

Greg: I agree that having different coaches would be good. Why not have all of our athletes go to a private a school?

Olivia: Most of us . . . can't afford stuff like that. If there are two teams, there are more opportunities . . . giving kids a chance to win college scholarships. The parents can't afford to send their kids to private or parochial schools.

Brady: I am a coach, and there is rivalry between coaches, too. . . . There is an ongoing problem. The coaches won't be happy because the athletes will continue to go to their own coaches.

Sarah: But are the two teams based on the schools or the skill level?

Brady: You are Oakdale coaches. Your coaches think that the Gresham athletes are not as good.

Shaun: I understand what you are saying. Most of Gresham is Mexican American. I want our teams to be the best. If it is based on skills, . . . Like Gresham has a history of success in soccer, so they will be a positive addition to the Oakdale teams.

Greg: The other teams have been the (reads) "conference doormats" for a long time. The kids who want to play volleyball and football, they will not have an equal chance. With two teams, there could be a healthy rivalry between the two teams.

Sarah (as teacher from Gresham): The students are comingling in one school. So how is that going to work when there are two teams in one school?

Shaun (as a neighborhood teen): If the kids from the Gresham neighborhood go home after practice and are wearing the Oakdale colors, they could be attacked in the neighborhood. (Cites *Brown v. Board of Education* to acknowledge that "separate but equal is not the best solution.") An option might be to merge the teams over time and . . . (describes a plan for gradual merger).

Greg: For any team to perform at a high level, there must be a feeling of solidarity . . .

Giorgio: Furthermore, there is a bigger picture here for the unity and the safety. When it is possible, change the colors of the schools so the colors could be blue and gold to have unity over time.

Shaun: It is going to be expensive. You have to change the uniforms and the colors in the gym. Being an athlete, you want your team to be the best. If you can make your team better, what would stop you from doing this? The only way for a coach to cut a player would be for the player to lack skill or discipline.

Greg: I understand, but the Oakdale coaches are very strong for Oakdale players so they only want players from Oakdale because they are prejudiced against Gresham. Separate teams would be best for preventing fights and . . .

Kassie: On the issue of funding, you would increase the costs if you have two separate teams. It would be best to merge the teams and the colors over time.

Paulie: I will lose my identity as a Gresham Monarch if you change the colors and merge the teams.

Olivia: As a parent, I need to send my kids off to college. Some parents are in poverty and can't afford to buy new equipment. As a parent, I would never want to see my kid not make the team. I think that there should still be two separate schools.

Paulie: I would rather that the Gresham athletes not merge. I am proud to be a Monarch and I don't think the Gresham athletes should try out at all. It is not loyal to Gresham because we would be playing for Oakdale.

THE TEACHER'S DIALOGIC MOVES

The productivity or functionality of the discussions depends a good deal on the structure of the inquiry activity itself; but much depends, obviously, on the moves of the teacher. The two discussion excerpts above reveal some basic elements of facilitating the discussion. The key perhaps is that Mr. Minton makes what Nystrand, Wu, Zeiser, Gamoran, and Long (2001) call a "dialogic bid" (p. 8). This bid might be the posing of a question that does not have a prespecified answer. In this case, Mr. Minton frames a problem. He notes the conflict at the heart of the case, but he also recognizes explicitly that the current discussions are part of a broader inquiry into tough perennial questions about one's sense of loyalty. In other words, he situates the current discussion in the larger context of an inquiry that will involve work with several texts, giving the current conversations significance and connections.

In many ways, Mr. Minton modeled the behavior that he wanted to foster among the learners. He acknowledged his own doubts about the issues, and he extended the conversation by involving all the students in one form of conversation or another. As he debriefed with the whole class, he paraphrased often to summarize the progress of the discussion and to elevate some contributions to the attention of the whole class. He extended discussion by referring to and building on students' contributions, and he asked appropriate follow-up questions to extend and clarify thinking. These moves in the large-group discussions model the behavior to guide the students' work in small groups throughout the term. The excerpts above represent two steps in a more involved process. Mr. Minton, like Ms. Edsel in Chapter 5, relies on the small-group work as a clearly exploratory experience and moves into the large-group discussion with the expectation that arguments are more fully formed and will include multiple perspectives. This showcasing of various points of view fosters further dialogue, because it acknowledges that answers regarding the issues are not static, but shifting and evolving.

One of the functions of Mr. Minton's paraphrasing in the large group is that it reveals not only the apparent points of agreement but also the remaining areas of doubt. It appears, and a later interview affirms, that he judges from moment to moment whether he needs to probe a particular student further, to summarize, to move to other contributors, or to bring the entire discussion to closure. He is also careful to keep the small-group and the large-group discussions connected to the long-term inquiry, which will include the reading of literary and other texts.

I noted earlier that in coding the discussions discussed in Chapter 5, a research assistant and I agreed on one instance when we could code a contribution as "social conversation." The fact that there was only one instance of "off-task" behavior struck us as exceptional. The situation was similar in the case of Mr. Minton's class. Perhaps the small sample of classes by chance included only students who were academically focused and unusually compliant with the teacher's directions. But I suspect that the students' engagement was the product of the way that the teacher prepared for and structured the activities. Here are the obvious elements of the preparation and execution:

- The teacher situated the discussions in the broader context: "Realize that our thinking today is part of a larger look at our sense of the importance of *loyalty*, or our sense of what it means to be loyal."

- The teacher planned for the grouping of students so that there would be built-in supports and diversity of thought within groups: that is, a student who could exercise leadership, both males and females, both shy and outgoing, and so on.
- The teacher planned for physical positioning of students so that they could face one another comfortably and different groups would not interfere with one another.
- The teacher set specific expectations for each discussion, by noting anticipated outcomes and setting guidelines, including a time limit: "You have the next 15 minutes to discuss in your groups, and then anyone in your group should be able to report to the rest of us what the assigned students, parents, coaches, or faculty members would have to say."
- The teacher provided a tangible and meaningful task, in that the students could project themselves into the narrative of the situation and could appreciate what the players in the circumstance cared about: "To appreciate how hard the situation is and the potential to encourage positive outcomes, you will talk in your groups about what various affected people would have to say."
- As students talked within their groups, the teacher moved around the room and visited groups to monitor the progress of the discussion, noting how each group was functioning as a team and checking for evidence that the exploratory talk was indeed preparing students to participate in the large-group forum.

These actions by the teacher and the thinking behind them are consistent with the practices that Hillocks, McCabe, and McCampbell (1971) long ago associated with "creating an environment for active learning" (p. 100). The teacher's "moves" to foster active learning in small groups prepared the learners to contribute to the large-group conversation. In initiating the large-group forum, Mr. Minton grounded the conversation in the context of the long-term inquiry into issues connected to the concept of *loyalty*. The questions about what the students and the community should do in regard to the problems associated with the closing of one school and the integration of students into another school obviously do not have pre-specified answers, which is essential to what Nystrand (1997) calls authentic discussion. To summarize what Ms. Edsel (Chapter 5) and Mr. Minton do, I suggest that the following are key "moves" for fostering authentic discussion that promotes the habits of thinking that are consistent with the Common Core State Standards for speaking and listening and are important for close reading and elaborated writing.

- The teacher connected the current conversation to the previous small-group discussion and to the long-range targets for the line of inquiry.
- The teacher solicited responses and paraphrased often, thus affirming contributions without endorsing "right" answers: "So the more gifted athletes have more at stake, but the other sports enthusiasts might lose out on a chance to play a sport they love, or at least to be associated with a team even if they don't play much."
- The teacher called on students to evaluate one another's contributions to the discussion: "Carolyn makes an interesting point, and I wonder if you agree."
- The teacher monitored the development of students' thinking, judging when follow-up questions were necessary and when it was time to introduce a new perspective.
- The teacher posed follow-up questions and possible exceptions: "How so?" "So, it is not so much a question of *loyalty* as it is a question of survival?"
- The teacher summarized the thread of the conversation and noted where the conversation needed to continue: "So far we have talked about how the students, especially athletes, might feel about the situation. But some of you thought about what the coaches would say. What did you conclude?"

The teachers described above ultimately moved students forward by connecting the current discussion to subsequent writing and reading. Mr. Minton, who expected students to write about the case they were discussing, wanted to see evidence that students were attending to the basic elements required in the written response. Here is how he prompted the written analysis:

WRITING ABOUT THE CASE

After you have discussed the case at length, you should be prepared to write to the appropriate audience to offer advice about the central question:

> What should the athletes from Gresham High School do about joining fall sports at Oakdale High? What can adults do to make the transition as safe and positive as possible?

You might want to write to a male or female athlete, to the Athletic Director at Oakdale, to the principal of Oakdale, or to the coaches from both schools. In any case, your written response should have the following elements:

An introduction: Even if your reader is familiar with the case, you will want to provide a brief summary of the situation and the problem. The summary should allow someone who is not familiar with the case to understand the central conflict. You also will want to express a position about the central question in the case.

A review of possible actions: As your class discussion probably revealed, everyone does not agree about what should happen. Review the arguments you have heard about the central question in the case. Explain why people have taken the positions that they have taken; but if you disagree, explain why you disagree with their reasoning.

An argument for your own position: Show your reader that after you have reviewed all possibilities, you have judged that, on balance, your recommendation is the best one. You should support any claims that you make, and explain any evidence that you offer by referring to established rules or principles. Your argument might show that your recommended course of action offers the greatest benefit and the fewest disadvantages.

A conclusion: To close your discussion, you will want to remind your readers about the issues involved in the case and reiterate your position.

Precision and propriety: The tone and appearance of your written response contributes to its persuasiveness. This means that the writing should be organized, logical, and coherent. This also means that mistakes in usage and punctuation should not cause confusion. Share a draft of your composition with another reader (e.g., classmate, family member, or friend) to check for correctness and clarity. Invite the reader also to comment on the tone of the writing: Do you "sound" appropriately respectful for the audience you are addressing? Use the feedback from your reader to edit your work and perhaps to revise it.

As the prompt suggests, Mr. Minton expected the students to learn a lot about *writing* by *talking*. In planning and monitoring the small- and large-group discussions, he looked for opportunities and evidence that students could frame the problem for an uninitiated reader, that they could form and support conclusions, that they could test evidence against the challenges of a skeptical audience, that they could interpret evidence for a reader, that they could report various perspectives accurately and evaluate them fairly, and that they could summarize a fairly long discussion and reiterate a position. The preparatory discussions were part of a longer composing process that included drafting, review, and refinement, with some attention to the requirement for "precision and propriety."

THE TEACHER'S THINKING BEHIND THE PRACTICE

From watching Mr. Minton teaching and from reviewing the transcripts of discussions in his class, a viewer can infer much about the thinking that drives his practice. To understand Mr. Minton's instructional practices, it is also useful to refer to his own reflections about why he does what he does from moment to moment and from lesson to lesson. Mr. Minton notes that he takes an "inquiry-based approach to writing instruction, one that emphasizes student-to-student dialogue." He feels a responsibility "to nurture classroom experiences that support an engaging and purposeful learning environment. I want students to actively experience what it means to develop questions, weigh evidence, and balance opposing viewpoints so that they are actively involved in creating the ideas that they will write about. I actively work against the tendency for students to look for the 'right' answer, or the answer they think their teacher wants them to develop. I want students to devise their own thoughts based on the way they refine their thinking through meaningful discussions with their peers." Mr. Minton's stated commitment to working against the simplicity of finding the "right" answer expresses the spirit of inquiry. Certainly the learners will have to be responsible for the accuracy of their reporting about texts and other sources of information, but Mr. Minton emphasizes that his primary goals are for the students to develop thought and command procedures, both of which benefit from the students' engaging with one another.

Mr. Minton notes that the observed discussions were part of a larger scheme to support students' inquiry into some compelling issues. He relies on discussions in almost every class meeting, and he frames each discussion in the context of a broader purpose:

> Our classroom discourse focuses on essential questions that guide our reading, and students use the context of these questions to develop their own understandings and to motivate them to write with purpose and effectiveness. For example, while reading *To Kill a Mockingbird*, students reflected on 'What's worth fighting for?' While reading *Lord of the Flies*, students inquired into the idea of *leadership* and developed a more refined understanding of what makes a good leader. In each case, students engaged in a series of discussions that helped them to refine their ideas and to apply them to their reading, a process that also assisted subsequent writings the students did in response to our reading.

This description of practice depicts an ongoing inquiry, with speaking and listening being important goals in themselves, but also planned in the service of writing and reading; and the study of a body of literary texts connected discussions and led to other elaborated writing.

Mr. Minton reports that his instructional approach has shifted since he first began teaching:

> When I first started teaching it seemed like it was easier for me to control and direct the class through more teacher-oriented activities, but I can't say I was very effective or that students were always engaged. Even now, while I dedicate all the time I can to supporting student interaction and meaningful talk, I don't hit a home run every day. But I am definitely more capable of structuring classroom discourse in a way that encourages students to take part and to make direct connections between the talking we do in class and improving literacy skills. So the best way to help students write better is get the students talking and learning in very purposeful and directed ways.

In short, Mr. Minton devotes a great deal of time to planning for students' interactions, with careful attention to the goals, structures, and sequence for the discussions; but in the classroom he relies on students to contribute often and to a certain extent to assume leadership. This approach to instruction does require that the teacher be confident enough to surrender some autonomy to the learners, and this confidence seems to be the product of practice and resiliency. Mr. Minton notes, "I'd advise them [beginning teachers] not to be shy about using adventuresome activities in class that allow students to do most of the talking and encourage students to openly participate and have a say in what is discussed." He also acknowledges that learners need to have an awareness of the dialogic processes in which they are engaged, with the teacher being responsible to prompt students to "reflect on how the thoughts generated in these discussions impact their reading and writing."

A STUDENT'S WRITTEN RESPONSE

Drawing from the discussions that Mr. Minton planned and facilitated, students were able to write elaborated compositions. The following excerpt is representative of the kind of responses that the students completed. The discussions served the student in knowing what questions a skeptical reader might have, and she drew from the written description of the case and the exchanges during discussions as sources of information to support her position and illustrate her generalizations.

Response to Gresham High Case

Anna Livingstone

Sports are very important to the students of Gresham High School and the faculty is guaranteeing a safe and positive transition into the new school, so it would only be reasonable if the athletes of Gresham try out for fall sports at Oakdale. There will be more opportunities for them at this new school without the requirement of money. Even though there is the fear of betraying their loyalty for Gresham students, the Gresham coaches believe "the Oakdale coaches and athletes have always had the advantage of better equipment, better facilities, and a larger talent pool" (page 3). These better facilities and equipment are a major improvement for the Gresham High School students, so this is a great opportunity for the Gresham athletes to improve their skills even more. The opportunity to improve their skills is imperative for Gresham athletes, because as the parents have stated, "They cannot not afford to send their children to private or parochial schools" (page 3). Based on the Gresham families' situation, this also implies that Gresham students could not afford to play on outside sports clubs or even afford college tuitions, so free sports opportunities from school and the chance of college scholarships are great resources to take advantage of while they are available.

The deans and faculty of Oakdale High are also making promises to the new transfers, as they say they " . . . in particular are committed to being proactive in resolving conflict and keeping the school peaceful" (page 4). The faculty recognizes that this merger could be a growing experience for the students of both high schools, but if any problems arise, they will be there to help and support those students in need, no matter which school they come from. It is always a better choice to recognize opportunities and take advantage of them while they last, because otherwise there will only be the feeling of regret, which makes no one a better person. The merger presents some major growing opportunities for the students of both high schools, as mergers like these can occur in the work world, too. The rivalry between students from the different schools may start off strong, but as the faculty has said, they will take care of any unnecessary violence; and by Gresham students participating in fall sports, students of both schools will need to work together in order to win, which is the usual desire of people for anything in life.

I have not reproduced the transcripts of the discussions across all of the groups in Mr. Minton's class, and I have not represented any discussion in its lengthy entirety. At the same time, the sample composition above reveals that the writer drew from the discussions. She refers explicitly to the discussions in class. The level of elaboration suggests that the exchanges during discussions emphasized a need to support her positions and to elaborate about that support. She reviews several positions—the athletes, other students, parents, coaches, and teachers—suggesting that the discussions represented in some detail the thoughts and feelings that these stakeholders might have in the controversy. Perhaps Anna was not an active contributor to the discussions, but, as Schultz (2009) suggests, she may have benefitted from her position as listener, attending to competing arguments and multiple points of view to work out her own position as she compares and contrasts it with the positions of the more vocal participants in the discussions. Although the teacher did not plan for an online extension to the discussion, Anna may have benefitted also from other discussion forums by way of email or social media. In the end, it does seem clear that Anna's writing benefitted from the inquiry and discussions.

EXTENDING THE INQUIRY AND DISCUSSION

Mr. Minton recognized that a good deal of significant literature depicts conflicts and demands related to *loyalty*. He expected that discussions, reading, and writing about the Gresham High case would help students in thinking about the tensions that characters in many works of literature experience. Here are some possibilities: *The Odyssey, Beowulf, The Tempest, All Quiet on the Western Front, The Informer, All the Pretty Horses,* "The Sniper," "Guests of the Nation," *Fallen Angels, The Hobbit* and *Lord of the Rings* trilogy, and the Harry Potter series. He also planned for more independent extensions to the work with the case, prompting students in this way:

> Many people think of *loyalty* as a positive trait. We might appreciate people who are loyal to their nation, to their family, to the company they work for, to their favorite team, to their city or region of the country, and so forth. All the same, loyalty can sometimes present problems—conflicts with people who are equally loyal to an opposing force, idea, or tradition; tensions between the loyalty to friends and the loyalty to family; dilemmas about the responsibilities to family and country and the perceived need to oppose some of their practices. Your own investigations can lead to deeper thinking and more elaborated, research-based writing.

This invitation to extending the inquiry recognizes that the students' thinking should not stop when an assignment is done and a grade assigned. Instead, if the students learn important procedures for thinking critically, for understanding the arguments of various contributors, and for advancing their own arguments, they should be aware of the procedures and should be able to apply them again in new situations.

Chapters 5, 6, and 7 feature high school teachers in action, but I see the same pattern of sequencing and expanding inquiry and discussion with some teachers and their classes in middle school and community college. In Chapter 8, I draw from the interviews with teachers to reveal across grades some common thinking that drives the teachers' broad planning and their decisions from episode to episode in individual lessons.

Expanding Dialogue

WHAT I'VE LEARNED FROM WATCHING
TEACHERS AND LEARNERS IN ACTION

I worked for years in public schools where part of my responsibility was to observe and evaluate teachers. I also have worked as a consultant to schools and as a university supervisor of student teachers. While serving in all of these roles, I have observed in hundreds of classrooms in a variety of different schools. I know from this experience that the teachers featured in this book are an exceptional bunch. I sought them out to observe and interview because colleagues whose judgment I value had identified the teachers as ones who were likely to emphasize inquiry and to foster a dialogic classroom. Several practices set them apart—their attention to specific learning goals and their related assessments, their planning for the cohesive unity of the curriculum, and their strategic sequencing of learning activities to scaffold from simple to complex, from dependence to independence. I know also that they are distinctive for nurturing a classroom environment where students are highly engaged and eager to participate in discussions. The teachers planned not only with attention to the specific outcomes that should result from the learning activities, but also with attention to the function of each learning activity and an awareness of how each discussion prepared the learners for the next one. The teachers knew what the function of each discussion was—what they should be able to hear and see among the learners—and referred to this identified function to judge whether students were demonstrating the kind of thinking that would support their writing and their study of connected texts. In the end, the teachers could judge whether students had command of the kind of procedures that would be important for their own independent efforts at research. These shared teacher attributes spanned from Grade 5 to community college.

I intended for the early working title of this book (i.e., *Expanding Dialogue*) to echo the important work of other researchers into the nature and impact of classroom discussions—Martin Nystrand's groundbreaking *Opening Dialogue* (1997) and Mary M. Juzwik, Carlin Borsheim-Black, Samantha Caughlan, and Anne Heintz's *Inspiring Dialogue* (2013). Nystrand noted that authentic discussions in schools are rare, which is an obvious pity when he reports that the frequency of authentic discussion correlates highly with achievement on measures of literacy. Juzwik et al. (2013) note the ways that teachers initiate and sustain authentic discussions, and the authors suggest specific practices for teachers to foster dialogue. The teachers that I observed for this book demonstrated time and again a sense of *expanding dialogue* based on principles of *inquiry*. The teachers' awareness of target outcomes guided their design of learning activities; but their appreciation of the complexity of the procedures associated with the target outcomes guided the teachers' strategic sequencing of discussion-based activities to build toward the instructional goals and to help learners to be aware of the procedures they were practicing. In the classrooms where I observed, the dialogue expanded—from initial exploratory efforts to drafting, synthesizing, and applying.

I was impressed that the teachers that I observed had a sense of the connections across a series of lessons that spanned weeks, and that the teachers could make the connections explicit for the learners, revealing that there was indeed a plan and that the plan involved all the students in collaborative investigation of compelling questions. Teachers were able to plan in a strategic way because they worked with a curriculum that they could represent to students as a unified whole. In this context, *strategic* means that the teachers had substantial end goals in mind and planned for a purposeful sequence of learning activities that would involve the students and move them inevitably toward the target learning outcomes. A 6th-grade teacher, who chose to be identified as Mrs. Soulis, noted her awareness of a broad plan: "The unit of inquiry for the 'at level' language arts class centered around the question of 'What makes a family a *good* family?' and for the advanced class, the question was, 'What are the qualities of a *true friendship*?' We started with the basics of writing a good definition so that the final paper could be an extended definition with criteria defining *friendship* or *family*." Mrs. Soulis reports that the process of defining involved a lot of discussion based on students' reactions to problem-based scenarios. The discussions were involved and took time: "After the small-group examination of the scenarios and development of criteria lists, there were good debates and suggestions for rewording. The discussions were lively; the lists were long and complex." The students then applied the criteria they derived through discussions to write definitions and to judge the families in *Maniac Magee* and the friendships depicted in *Roll of Thunder, Hear My Cry*. The teacher carefully organized the sequence, drawing on students' knowledge about defining, complicating the process by presenting problem situations to invite refinement (e.g., "debates" and "rewording"), and then applying the refined framework to judging characters and situations in the literature the 6th-graders discussed.

Similarly, a community college teacher, Ms. Peterdale, noted that she relied on "inquiry-based prewriting, discussing in pairs and subsequently as a whole class." I observed Ms. Peterdale as she worked with a "developmental" first-year composition class. Part of her strategy for preparing students to examine texts and to write college-level essays included introductory, exploratory activities leading to "discussing ideas and opinions for drafting, peer reviewing, instructor reviewing, and revising." She explains the importance she places on the discussions: "The interactions that students have in class serve to create a dynamic learning community. Students also learn from each other how to add to their own ideas and to use sources and each other to add substance to their papers. We also use discussion to understand alternative viewpoints and learn to incorporate these viewpoints perhaps as a counterargument in one's own writing."

The teachers that I observed for this book were skilled practitioners, and they worked on the craft of facilitating discussions. They also orchestrated opportunities for students to interact with one another, without the intrusion of the teacher to do the analysis and to affirm answers.

The teachers acknowledge that they work at protecting a dialogic classroom, sometimes catching themselves talking too much and taking command of the procedures that the learners should be practicing, but then correcting themselves to make sure that all learners are involved in the learning activities. As Hillocks (1999) reports, the teachers' beliefs about the ways that students learn guide the teachers' practice. Mrs. Soulis, the 6th-grade teacher, noted, "I believe students learn by thinking deeply, talking things through, continuing to grapple with the same basic inquiry question for an extended period from a variety of angles." In order to influence learners to think deeply and grapple with questions, Mrs. Soulis had to monitor her own commitment to an inquiry process and had to frame for learners the kind of compelling problems that would involve them in discussions that affirmed for them that they did know something and that they could talk intelligently with peers about what they knew. Referring to prescribed topics from a literacy series that her school district had adopted, Mrs. Soulis observed: "Having them write about bat extermination in South America? They don't know bats so well. So then they struggle understanding the content and how to write about it. And they don't really care very much about school uniforms, homework policies, or cell phones in school, unless these things are *really* being debated in your district. Every standardized test uses these sorry excuses for debatable topics anyway." In contrast, her 6th-graders knew much about friendship and family, and they cared about how they and others judged the quality of friendship and family, which elevated the significance of the inquiry and discussions.

Similarly, Ms. Peterdale, the community college teacher, urges teachers to know their students well and build from this knowledge. She advises a new teacher to

> help her students have an entry point into reading a text, with, for example, prewriting that includes students' experiences with the theme, topic, subject to be explored in the upcoming unit of instruction. Validate the students' opinions and analysis by listening and encouraging further analysis, through discussion with pairs, small groups, and the whole class. Engage in critical thinking, especially by discussing with peers and considering alternative points of view, considerations that test students' assumptions. In the end, insist that students *do* have something to say about most any topic we discuss and write about in class. In this way, the teacher validates her students' authentic voices and encourages further improvement and advancement of critical reading, thinking, and writing skills.

I judge that the teachers I observed not only connected the series of related discussions, but they had a sense of expanding the inquiry. This was most obvious when the investigation involved argument. Initially, discussions helped students to probe and stumble a bit as they sought to understand how they felt about the focus of the inquiry and discovered what their classmates thought. As the process advanced, the students drew from one another to construct their own arguments and to evaluate the arguments of others. The students also drew from the reading of related articles, including their classmates' reporting about what they had read. The talk about the readings involved summarizing and connecting. The teachers' plans projected that the students would apply the thinking that they practiced while talking to peers to their understanding and critical assessment of selected literature. Furthermore, equipped with procedures for framing a problem, situating an argument, summarizing and evaluating the arguments of others, and connecting a series of related arguments, including those represented in texts, the learners would be able to follow their own inquiry path, applying the same procedures in other classes or on other occasions in the English class, and in pursuit of answers to the questions they generated themselves.

SOME FINAL THOUGHTS

The teachers featured in this book are a special group and unlikely to represent what most teachers do to involve students in discussions that are integral to inquiry and that prepare learners for writing elaborated compositions. I rely on a small sample because I sought to observe teachers who strategically use discussions as a key part of the preparation for writing. Rarely do teachers foster authentic discussion (Juzwik et al., 2013; Nystrand, 1997), and rarely do teachers rely on extensive discussions as part of the preparation for writing (Applebee & Langer, 2006, 2011, 2013). These trends do not have to persist. The teachers featured in this book offer models for how to transform classrooms to be more dialogic, and teaching and learning to be more inquiry-based. Future research might draw from a broader pool of teachers to generalize about discussion practices that foster dialogue, advance inquiry, and prepare students to write elaborated and logical compositions. But the examples in this book suggest that students learn much from discussions that invite them to engage in procedures that also serve them in their writing of elaborated compositions and position them to enter into other critical dialogues about the texts they study together.

It probably strikes a lot of experienced teachers as obvious that all discussions are not the same; but this has been a significant finding of my work with teachers from 5th grade through college. As I hope the featured instructors illustrate, some teachers who emphasize inquiry plan discussions strategically, in anticipation that specific discussions will foster engagement in specific procedures. In turn, the learning of procedures from one discussion prepares learners for engagement in the next discussions. For these teachers, the discussions are not a set of intellectual silos, but a dialogic network that extends thinking, encourages command of procedures for problem solving and composing, and deepens understanding of significant issues. The emphasis in this book has been on the preparation for writing, especially for the writing of argument. It would be revealing to track these teachers and others like them as they follow the line of inquiry into the exploration of literature and into students' more independent efforts at investigation of critical issues. It would be revealing also to follow the ways in which students extend discussions through digital means such as wiki environments, email, or social media.

I judge that many teachers would benefit from looking closely at the practices of teachers like Ms. Boski and Ms. Wieczorek in 5th grade; Mrs. Soulis in 6th grade; Ms. Edsel and Mr. Minton in high school; and Ms. Peterdale in a community college. The brief summaries in Chapter 7 of Mr. Minton's "moves" and his commentary on the thinking that guides him are likely to serve teachers well in thinking about ways to extend their own classroom discourse into a more dialogic mode. While the summaries in this book feature high school teachers, I have observed that the teachers in 5th grade, 6th grade, and a community college follow similar practices. Taken together, the practices of all the teachers featured in this book offer promise that dialogue is possible, and that most learners thrive in a dialogic

environment and become more confident and capable speakers and writers and more mature, reflective readers. In addition, the experience with
grappling with one another immerses learners in the essentially democratic
habits of joining critical conversations—attending to competing perspectives, lending voice in seeking understanding and improvement, and working toward collaborative solutions.

Appendixes

Scenarios: How Are We Obligated?

Directions: In order to consider the extent to which an individual is responsible for others, we first must determine a procedure for judging the extent of one's *obligation* toward others. The following scenarios depict several conflicts between various individuals and among members of a community. In your groups, determine the following: (1) the nature of the relationship depicted in the scenario, (2) the costs and benefits of possible decisions, and (3) your judgment about the specific decision the individual should make. Please explain why and cite specific evidence when crafting your arguments.

1. Robert Cunningham is a creature of habit. For 30 years, he has worked at the New York City Police Department as a well-respected and honest detective. During the course of those years, Detective Cunningham developed specific behaviors that he stays true to from week to week. For example, every morning he wakes up at 6 A.M. to make his wife breakfast, drink his coffee, and read *The New York Times*. When Detective Cunningham works the night shift on Tuesdays and Thursdays, he always stops into Sal's Pizzeria in nearby Yonkers, NY, for dinner. He always sits at the same table, orders the linguini and clam sauce, and converses with the same waitress, Phyllis Penzo. One day, upon forgetting his wallet, Detective Cunningham offers Phyllis a deal: Instead of paying for the meal and the tip, the pair share the lottery ticket that Detective Cunningham bought earlier that day. If they win, they split the $3 million jackpot 50/50. Phyllis agrees, and Detective Cunningham watches the Powerball drawing the next day. He watches the television with bated breath. In an unbelievable turn of events, Detective Cunningham jumps out of his recliner in a fit of excitement; he has the winning ticket. Although the agreement between the detective and Phyllis is verbal with no

137

handshake, should Detective Cunningham still hold up his end of the bargain?

2. Jenni and Kristi have been friends since 4th grade. Although they have had some ups and downs, they still remain the best of friends. Furthermore, the pair feels as though they're more like sisters instead of just friends, and they would do anything for each other. Lately, Jenni has been having trouble with their mutual friend, Alicia. When Kristi and Alicia hang out, Jenni is rarely invited and frequently bad-mouthed by Alicia. On the rare occasion that Jenni is invited, if Jenni cannot make it due to family and school conflicts, Alicia calls her a bad friend. This pattern of behavior has gone on for quite some time, but so far, Kristi has chosen not to intervene. As time passes, Jenni is becoming more and more upset and hurt and asks Kristi to say something to Alicia, but Kristi still "doesn't want to get in the middle of it." What should Kristi do?

3. Mike and Sam are doing a group project for their world language class. The project that they are doing is called "Taking Spanish to the Streets" and it consists of three parts. The first part is the practical that involves going to a Mexican grocery store and speaking only in Spanish to the store employees. After they have completed the practical portion of the project, they are then supposed to make authentic Latino or Spanish food to bring to the class. Once they have completed parts one and two, they are each responsible for writing a one-page reflection about their experience. They have decided to do the shopping and the cooking together and write the reflection separately. When Sam goes to the Mexican grocery store to meet with Mike to go shopping, Mike never shows, and Sam has to do all the shopping by himself. The next day for the cooking portion, Mike sends Sam a text explaining that something came up and he is unable to cook. What is Sam's obligation to Mike?

4. To the students and faculty at Trinity High School, football is not just a game but a way of life. Football is so embedded into the culture of the school that nearly everyone in the town shows up to the game on Friday night. So far, the Lions have had a perfect season, and Coach Douglas wants to keep it that way. Accordingly, he prepares extensively for each and every single game. While scouting out the Gainesville State School Panthers, the team of juvenile delinquents from Gainesville Detention Center, he knows that the Lions will easily win because the Panthers are a newly established team and they are not nearly as cohesive as a team. Plus, the Lions have home field advantage as well as a very strong fan base. However, while watching the game, Coach Douglas observes that there are no fans in the

Panthers' stands. In fact, many of the parents of the players probably have disowned them. It is clear that many of the Gainesville players are trying very hard to make a fresh start, and Coach Douglas begins to sympathize with them. He thinks to himself, "What if there was some way to support their rehabilitation during the game between the Lions and the Panthers? Maybe we could give them half of our fans so that they have some people at the game to cheer them on." Even though the Panthers are the opposing team, should Coach Douglas give them moral support?

5. Mr. Hennesey's math class is definitely one of the most difficult classes at Gompers East High School. While he is good teacher, his expectations for his students are high. As a teacher, Mr. Hennesey is a tough grader who always emphasizes to his students the importance of taking notes. In fact, notes are 30% of the students' grade. So far in the quarter, William Jenkins has attended each of Mr. Hennesey's classes and has taken very detailed notes during every class meeting. One day, 15 minutes after the bell, Jonathan Swanson, a student who rarely shows up to class, leans over and asks William if he can borrow the notes from the past three classes. William is caught off guard, but what should he do?

6. Privates Thornton and Woods have been together since joining the army straight out of high school. They met in boot camp where they were assigned to the same squad and endured many hardships brought on by intense training and strict rules. They instantly became friends. Even when they were granted weekend liberty, they always went out on the town together to have fun. When it came time to be deployed, the two were lucky enough to be assigned to the same battalion in Iraq. Upon arriving in "The Sandbox," the men realized that their friendship would be tested. After narrowly escaping an IED (improvised explosive device) explosion that left a member of the battalion without a leg, Private Woods made an imploring request to his best friend. Private Woods judged that losing a limb would be absolutely devastating and would ruin his life and any chances he ever had at a successful military career. So, he asked Private Thornton to "finish the job." Should Thornton "finish the job"?

7. The Nosce brothers, Timothy and Sage, have always shared a special connection. Although they are identical twins, you would not be able to tell. Due to complications during their birth, Sage was born with both a club foot and a mild learning disability, while Timothy was born without any physical or mental disabilities. Throughout Timothy's and Sage's childhood, the two were referred to as a "package deal" because they were always together. As the twins grew older, Timothy began to

advance in mental development, while Sage stayed the same. Timothy thinks that his brother is capable of keeping up with the other kids and is embarrassed that he has to look after Sage all the time. Timothy wants to help his brother improve in cognitive skills, but feels like he is being selfish. What should Timothy do?

APPENDIX B: METHODS FOR CODING CLASSROOM DISCOURSE

A research assistant transcribed all of the recordings collected from classroom discussions. I developed a system of codes (see Appendix C), based on hundreds of hours of observations of classroom activities and in anticipation of the utterances that one was likely to hear in discussions designed to prepare students for writing an extended definition essay. For the purposes of our coding, the length of the utterance could vary, depending on the function of the contribution to the discussion. For example, a claim could be a brief sentence or a fragment; the citing of data could be a paragraph long. A research assistant and I applied the codes independently to the sets of transcripts. By checking for agreement across the sets of codes, we clarified the codes themselves and agreed on their application.

After the research assistant and I refined the coding system, the research assistant trained two other graduate students who were not familiar with the study. Following an initial training session with a set of common transcripts and establishing a high level of inter-rater reliability, the two graduate students continued to code the transcripts independently. The research assistant checked inter-rater reliability three times during the process, with agreement percentages of 86.4, 95, and 86, and a total reliability level of 88.6%.

Since the length of the discussions varied, I report the data in percentages rather than as tallies (see Appendix D); the percentages are a more revealing indicator of the nature of the discussions. I judge that, as an example, the reporting of eight instances of citing data would be less meaningful than knowing that that number represented 30% of the total contributions to the discussion. Eight utterances might be the same percentage of all contributions, whether the discussion were 15 minutes or 25 minutes. The data from coding the discussions appear in Appendix D and in Figures 5.1–5.6 in Chapter 5. For the purposes of reporting the data, I have included only the codes that reveal the substance of the discussion. Although we coded for utterances related to procedures for the activity (e.g., "What are we supposed to be doing again?"), for clarifying attempts (e.g., "What did you say?"), and for fragmentary utterances (e.g., "Uh, uh, . . ." or "My sister always . . ."), these instances do not appear in the summaries. These coded elements help to reveal the dynamics of the group, but reveal little about the substance of the conversation as it might support the subsequent composing of an academic essay.

APPENDIX C: CODES FOR CLASSROOM DISCUSSIONS

C: *making a claim:* The speaker asserts a claim (i.e., conclusion, generalization) relative to the focus for the discussion.

D: *citing support for claim:* The speaker offers some form of data (e.g., actual or invented example, reference to a statement by an authority, statistical data, information) to support a claim.

W: *explaining/interpreting support for claim:* The speaker explains the connection between expressed support and a claim. To connect claim and support, the speaker might cite a rule of thumb, a law of nature, a statute of government, an ethical principle, or a rule of an organization, like a school.

B: *backing the interpretation:* The speaker cites support to suggest the legitimacy of a warrant or interpretation of data.

H: *challenging/questioning a claim:* The speaker challenges the claim, the accuracy or relevance of the support, or the legitimacy of a principle used to interpret support.

A: *anticipating opposing argument:* The speaker acknowledges expressed or anticipated opposition.

R: *reiterating a claim:* The speaker restates or affirms the claim expressed by a speaker in the group.

U: *summarizing a portion of the discussion:* The speaker summarizes what has been said as a means for affirming the status of the discussion. The summary involves more than the paraphrase of a single speaker.

P: *noting procedures for the discussion:* The speaker asks a procedural question or otherwise clarifies the task for the group. The speaker prompts others about some aspect of the task, including the reading from the material that has prompted the discussion.

S: *socializing:* The speaker makes a strictly social comment that does not appear to contribute to the progress of the discussion.

L: *clarifying:* The speaker checks for understanding or affirms understanding, especially about what a conversational partner has said. This category includes a teacher's simple paraphrase of a speaker's contribution.

F: *uttering a fragmentary comment:* The speaker offers a fragmentary statement, the purpose of which is unclear.

APPENDIX D: PERCENTAGES OF CONTRIBUTIONS TO DISCUSSIONS

	Claim	Data	Warrant	Backing	Challenge	Anticipate	Reiterate	Summarize	Socialize
Small group: survey	35.56	28.89	8.89	0.00	4.44	0.00	20.00	1.48	0.74
Large group: survey	14.67	32.00	17.33	4.00	10.67	1.33	13.33	6.67	0.00
Large group: teacher models scenario	23.40	34.04	23.40	0.00	6.38	0.00	12.77	0.00	0.00
Small group: scenarios	26.25	17.50	16.25	1.25	21.25	0.00	17.50	0.00	0.00
Large group: scenarios	35.06	23.38	18.18	0.00	6.49	0.00	15.58	1.30	0.00
Small group: remaining scenarios	12.64	26.44	20.69	1.15	8.05	0.00	24.14	0.00	6.90

APPENDIX E: STUDENT INTERVIEW QUESTIONS

1. Do you like to write? What is it that you like or don't like?
2. Do you usually get good grades or good comments on the kind of compositions that you write in school?
3. If you have not received good grades in the past, how would you explain your good grades or comments this year?
4. When you have to write a fairly long composition (i.e., more than one page) in school, how do feel about completing the writing assignment?
5. When you have to write a composition for school, what helps you?
6. I see that this year you wrote some long compositions. If you think about one of the compositions you wrote, what helped you to write as much as you did? (directions? involvement in discussions? work with a partner or partners? printed material? the standard of grading? a conference with the teacher?)
7. What advice do you have for students who want to write very good compositions for this class next year? What do these students need to do to write high-quality, elaborated compositions?

APPENDIX F: TEACHER INTERVIEW QUESTIONS

1. How would you describe the approach you have followed for writing instruction this year?
2. What beliefs about how students learn underlie your approach to writing instruction?
3. What evidence do you have that your students have grown as writers this year?
4. What instructional experiences do you think had the greatest impact on the quality of students' writing this year?
5. In the activities that you used to prepare students for writing extended compositions, the students interacted frequently with one another. What function do you think these interactions served?
6. What advice would offer for a new teacher who wants to have a positive impact on students' learning to write well?

APPENDIX G: SAMPLES OF DEBATABLE CASES IN THE NEWS

Focus/ Emphasis	Case	Problem	Sample Related Literature
Must we obey authority?	"Build a Wiffle Ball Field and the Lawyers Will Come," *New York Times*, July 10, 2008	Would teens be justified in violating a city ordinance?	*Things Fall Apart* *The Giver* "Letter from Birmingham Jail" *The Night Thoreau Spent in Jail* "Essay on Civil Disobedience" *The Adventures of Huckleberry Finn*
What is honor?	"Judge Is Asked to Let 2 Join Honor Group," *New York Times*, November 27, 1998	Do these students deserve to be classified as "honor students"?	*To Kill a Mockingbird* *The Odyssey* *Julius Caesar* *All the Pretty Horses*
Are we free to choose?	"Health Panel Approves Restriction on Sale of Large Sugary Drinks," *New York Times*, September 13, 2012	Do we have a right to choose our own behavior, even if it is dangerous or unhealthy?	*Anthem* *The Hunger Games* *The Dispossessed* (Le Guin) *Native Son* *On Liberty*
What is justice?	"Tale of Dead Texas Dog Bites Mayor Who Told It," *New York Times*, February 13, 2008	How do we respond to reprehensible behavior?	*King Lear* *Native Son* *Monster* (W.D. Myers) *Roll of Thunder, Hear My Cry* (Taylor) *Warriors Don't Cry* (Beals)
What do we value most?	"Worker Who Hid Lottery Win Must Share $38.5 Million Prize," *New York Times*, March 14, 2012	What values guide our decisions?	*The Pearl* *Treasure of Sierra Madre* *Great Expectations* *Great Gatsby* *The Piano Lesson* (Wilson)

APPENDIX G: SAMPLES OF DEBATABLE CASES IN THE NEWS *(CONTINUED)*

Focus/ Emphasis	Case	Problem	Sample Related Literature
What is maturity?	"Youth Driving Laws Limit Even the Double Date," *New York Times*, August 13, 2012	What is maturity, and how does a person attain it?	*To Kill a Mockingbird* *House on Mango Street* *The Color of Water* (McBride) *Hope in the Unseen* (Suskind) *Catcher in the Rye*
What is the balance between privacy and security?	"Mapping, and Sharing, the Consumer Genome," *New York Times*, June 16, 2012 "Keeping Loved Ones on the Grid," *New York Times*, October 22, 2012 "Private Snoops Find GPS Trail Legal to Follow," January 28, 2012	To what extent should parents, authorities, and businesses be able to monitor our behavior?	*1984* *Brave New World* *The Giver* *Fahrenheit 451* "Harrison Bergeron" (Vonnegut)
How do you define identity, and how is an accurate sense of identity important?	"Case Pits Adoptive Parents Against Tribal Rights," *New York Times*, December 24, 2012	What factors define our identity? Who gets to define who we are? To what extent is it important that we know who we are?	*The House on Mango Street* *The Absolutely True Diary of a Part-Time Indian* *The Color of Water* *The Light in the Forest*
How do you decide whether to be vengeful or merciful?	"Before Escape, Fleeting Clues to Long Ordeal," *New York Times*, May 7, 2013	What is the appropriate response to serious harms to ourselves and to those we care about?	*The Merchant of Venice* *Night* *The Diary of Ann Frank* *King Lear* *Wuthering Heights*

APPENDIX G: SAMPLES OF DEBATABLE CASES IN THE NEWS *(CONTINUED)*

Focus/ Emphasis	Case	Problem	Sample Related Literature
To what extent can we trust our perceptions of others?	"John Demjanjuk, 91, Dogged by Charges of Atrocities as Nazi Camp Guard, Dies," *New York Times*, March 17, 2012	How can we be sure that we know what we think we know?	*Emma* *Pride and Prejudice* *Harry Potter* series *Much Ado About Nothing* *Measure for Measure*
What is a more perfect community?	"Gates Calls for a Final Push to Eradicate Polio," *New York Times*, January 31, 2011	How close can we come to forming an ideal society? Is it futile to try for the ideal?	*The Ones Who Walk Away from Omelas* *I Have a Dream* *Utopia* "Harrison Bergeron" *The Prince*
What are the limits of freedom of expression?	"Glenbrook South Athletes to Write Apology Over Flag," *Chicago Tribune*, October 14, 2003 "Ruling 'Bong Hits' Out of Bounds, *Time*, June 25, 2007	What are the limits, if any, to freedom of expression? Why would it be important to protect freedom of expression?	*1984* *Fahrenheit 451* *Animal Farm* *Nothing But the Truth* *The Giver*
What does it mean to be loyal?	"After 88 Years of Rivalry, the Last as Us and Them," *New York Times*, November 22, 2007 "An Involuntary Union of Football Rivals for Philadelphia High Schools," *New York Times*, August 3, 2013	To whom do you owe your loyalty? How important is loyalty? Can you divide your loyalties?	*Guests of the Nation* *The Informer* *Othello* *Song of Solomon* *The Outsiders* *The Kite Runner*

References

Ahmed-Ullah, N. S., Chase, J. & Secter, R. (2013, May 23). CPS approves largest school closure in Chicago's history. *Chicago Tribune*. Available at chicagotribune. com

Applebee, A. N. (1981). *Writing in the secondary schools*. Urbana, IL: National Council of Teachers of English.

Applebee, A. N. (1986). Problems in process approaches: Toward a reconceptualization of process instruction. In A. R. Petrosky & D. Bartholomae (Eds.), *The teaching of writing, 85th yearbook of the National Society for the Study of Education* (pp. 95–113). Chicago, IL: University of Chicago Press.

Applebee, A. N., & Langer, J. A. (2006). *The state of writing instruction in America's schools: What existing data tell us*. Albany, NY: State University of New York at Albany, National Research Center on English Learning & Achievement.

Applebee, A. N., & Langer, J. A. (2011). EJ extra: A snapshot of writing instruction in middle schools and high schools. *English Journal, 100*(6), 14–27.

Applebee, A. N., & Langer, J. A. (2013). *Writing instruction that works: Proven methods for middle and high school classrooms*. New York, NY: Teachers College Press.

Applebee, A. N., Langer, J. A., Nystrand, M., & Gamoran, A. (2003, Fall). Discussion-based approaches to developing understanding: Classroom instruction and student performance in middle and high school English. *American Educational Research Journal, 40*(3), 685–730.

Atwell, N. (1998). *In the middle: New understanding about writing, reading, and learning* (2nd ed.). Portsmouth, NH: Heinemann.

Barnes, D. (1992). *Communication to curriculum*. Portsmouth, NH: Heinemann.

Barnes, D. (2008). Exploratory talk for learning. In N. Mercer & S. Hodgkinson (Eds.), *Exploring talk in school* (pp. 1–16). Thousand Oaks, CA: Sage.

Burke, J. (2010). *What's the big idea? Question-driven units to motivate reading, writing, and thinking*. Portsmouth, NH: Heinemann.

Collins, J. (1982). Discourse style, classroom interaction and differential treatment. *Journal of Reading Behavior, 14*, 429–437.

Common Core State Standards Initiative. (2010). *English language arts standards*. Available at www.corestandards.org/ELA-Literacy

Daniels, H., & Zemelman, S. (1988). *A community of writers: Teaching writing in the junior and senior high school.* Portsmouth, NH: Heinemann.

Dewey, J. (1938). *Logic: The theory of inquiry.* New York, NY: Henry Holt.

Emig, J. (1971). *The composing processes of twelfth graders* (NCTE Research Rep. No. 13). Urbana, IL: National Council of Teachers of English.

Fecho, B. (2011). *Writing in the dialogical classroom: Students and teachers responding to the texts of their lives.* Urbana, IL: National Council of Teachers of English.

Gee, J. P. (2007). *What video games have to teach us about learning and literacy* (2nd ed., rev. and updated ed.). New York, NY: Palgrave Macmillan.

Gevinson, S., Hammond, D., & Thompson, P. (2006). *Increase the peace: A program for ending school violence.* Portsmouth, NH: Heinemann.

Goodlad, J. (1984). *A place called school: Prospects for the future.* New York, NY: McGraw-Hill.

Graff, G. (2004). *Clueless in academe: How schooling obscures the life of the mind.* New Haven, CT: Yale University Press.

Graham, S., & Perin, D. (2007a). What we know, what we still need to know: Teaching adolescents to write. *Scientific Studies of Reading, 11*(4), 313–335.

Graham, S., & Perin, D. (2007b). *Writing next: Effective strategies to improve writing of adolescents in middle and high schools.* New York, NY: Carnegie Corporation.

Graves, D. H. (1983). *Writing: Teachers and children at work.* Portsmouth, NH: Heinemann.

Hillocks, G., Jr. (1982). The interaction of instruction, teacher comment, and revision in teaching the composing process. *Research in the Teaching of English, 16*(3), 261–278.

Hillocks, G., Jr. (1984). What works in teaching composition: A meta-analysis of experimental treatment studies. *American Journal of Education, 93*(1), 133–170.

Hillocks, G., Jr. (1986a). *Research on written composition: New directions for teaching.* Urbana, IL: ERIC/NCRE.

Hillocks, G., Jr. (1986b). The writer's knowledge: Theory, research, and implications for practice. In A. R. Petrosky & E. Bartholomae (Eds.), *The teaching of writing, 85th yearbook of the National Society for the Study of Education* (pp. 71–94). Chicago, IL: University of Chicago Press.

Hillocks, G., Jr. (1999). *Ways of thinking, ways of teaching.* New York, NY: Teachers College Press.

Hillocks, G., Jr. (2002). *The testing trap: How state writing assessments control learning.* New York, NY: Teachers College Press.

Hillocks, G., Jr. (2011). *Teaching argument writing, grades 6–12: Supporting claims with relevant evidence and clear reasoning.* Portsmouth, NH: Heinemann.

Hillocks, G., Jr., Kahn, E., & Johannessen, L. (1983). Teaching defining strategies as a mode of inquiry. *Research in the Teaching of English, 17,* 275–284.

Hillocks, G., Jr., McCabe, B., & McCampbell, J. (1971). *The dynamics of English instruction, grades 7–12.* New York, NY: Random House.

Hu, W. (2007, November 22). After 88 years of rivalry, the last of us and them. *New York Times.* Available at www.nytimes.com

Johnson, T. S., Thompson, L., Smagorinsky, P., & Fry, P. G. (2003, November). Learning to teach the five-paragraph theme. *Research in the Teaching of English, 38*(2), 136–176.

Juzwik, M. M., Borsheim-Black, C., Caughlan, S., & Heintz, A. (2013). *Inspiring dialogue: Talking to learn in the English classroom.* New York, NY: Teachers College Press.

Langer, J. A. (2001, Winter). Beating the odds: Teaching middle and high school students to read and write well. *American Education Research Journal, 38*(4), 837–880.

Logman, J. (2013, August 3). An involuntary union of football rivals for Philadelphia high schools. *New York Times.* Available at www.nytimes.com

Macrorie, K. (1986). *Writing to be read.* Portsmouth, NH: Heinemann.

Macrorie, K. (1996). *Uptaught.* Portsmouth, NH: Heinemann.

McCann, T. M. (2011). Teaching English as a subversive activity. *English Journal, 101*(2), 90–92.

McCann, T. M., D'Angelo, R., Hillocks, M., Galas, N., & Ryan, L. (2012). Exploring character through narrative, drama, and argument. *English Journal, 101*(6), 37–43.

McCann, T. M., Johannessen, L. R., Kahn, E., & Flanagan, J. (2006). *Talking in class: Using discussion to enhance teaching and learning.* Urbana, IL: National Council of Teachers of English.

McCleary, W. C. (1979). Teaching deductive logic: A test of the Toulmin and Aristotelian models for critical thinking and college composition. *DAI, 40,* 1247.

Meier, D. (1995). *The power of their ideas.* Boston, MA: Beacon Press.

Murray, D. (2003). *A writer teaches writing* (Rev. 2nd ed.). Boston, MA: Thomson Heinle.

Newmann, F. M., Marks, H. M., & Gamoran, A. (1996, August). Authentic pedagogy and student performance. *American Journal of Education, 104,* 280–312.

Nussbaum, M. C. (1997). *Cultivating humanity: A classical defense of reform in liberal education.* Cambridge, MA: Harvard University Press.

Nystrand, M. (1997). *Opening dialogue: Understanding the dynamics of language and learning in the English classroom.* New York, NY: Teachers College Press.

Nystrand, M., Wu, L. L., Zeiser, S., Gamoran, A., & Long, D. (2001). Questions in time: Investigating the structure and dynamics of unfolding classroom discourse (Rep. Series 14005). Albany, NY: State University of New York at Albany, National Research Center on English Learning & Achievement. Available at www.albany.edu/cela/reports/nystrand/nystrandquestions14005.pdf

Schultz, K. (2009). *Rethinking classroom participation: Listening to silent voices.* New York, NY: Teachers College Press.

Smagorinsky, P. (2007). *Teaching English by design.* Portsmouth, NH: Heinemann.

Smagorinsky, P., & Fly, P. K. (1993, April). The social environment of the classroom: A Vygotskian perspective on small group process. *Communication Education, 42*(2), 159–171.

Smagorinsky, P., & Fly, P. K. (1994, March). A new perspective on why small groups do and don't work. *English Journal, 83*(3), 54–58.

Smagorinsky, P., Johannessen, L. R., Kahn, E. E., & McCann, T. M. (2010). *The dynamics of writing instruction: A structured process approach for middle school and high school.* Portsmouth, NH: Heinemann.

Smagorinsky, P., Johannessen, L. R., Kahn, E. E., & McCann, T. M. (2011). *Teaching students to write argument.* Portsmouth, NH: Heinemann.

Smith, M. W., & Wilhelm, J. (2007). *Getting it right: Fresh approaches to teaching grammar, usage, and correctness.* New York, NY: Scholastic, Inc.

Smith, M. W., Wilhelm, J. D., & Fredricksen, J. E. (2012). *Oh, yeah?! Putting argument to work both in school and out.* Portsmouth, NH: Heinemann.

Stern, D. E. (1994). *Teaching English so it matters.* Thousand Oaks, CA: Corwin Press.

Troyka, L. Q. (1974). *A study of the effect of simulation-gaming on expository prose competence of college remedial English composition students* (Doctoral dissertation, New York University). (ERIC Document Reproduction Service No. ED 090 541)

VanDerHeide, J., & Newell, G. E. (2013, July). Instructional chains as a method for examining the teaching and learning of argumentative writing in classrooms. *Written Communication, 30*(3), 300–329.

Vygotsky, L. (1978). *Mind in society: The development of higher cognitive processes.* Boston, MA: Harvard University Press.

Vygotsky, L. (1986). *Thought and language.* Boston, MA: MIT Press.

Weaver, C. (1996). *Teaching grammar in context.* Portsmouth, NH: Heinemann.

Wiggins G., & McTighe, J. (2005). *Understanding by design* (2nd ed.). Alexandria, VA: Association for Supervision and Curriculum Development.

Williams, J. M. (2004). *Problems into PROBLEMS: A rhetoric of motivation.* Fort Collins, CO: The WAC Clearinghouse. Available at wac.colostate.edu/books/williams/williams.pdf

Index

Large-group discussions *(continued)*
  inquiry into definition, 83–85, 87,
    91, 92, 93
  inquiry into narrative, 8–10
  progressively more complicated, 51
  student participation in, 43
  teacher role in, 87, 88–90
Logic (Dewey), 27
Logical writing, of community college
    students, 5
Logman, Jere, 111, 116
Long, D., 121
"Loyal to You, Gresham High" (case),
    112–130
  dialogic moves of teacher, 121–125
  discussing the case, 117–121
  statement of case, 112–116
  student written response to case,
    127–129
  teaching thinking behind
    instructional practice, 125–127
  working with the case, 116–117
  writing about the case, 124–125

Macrorie, K., 3
Marks, H. M., 17–18, 111, 117
McCabe, B., 123
McCampbell, J., 123
McCann, T. M., 6, 7, 22, 24, 51, 59,
    65, 117
McCleary, W. C., 4–6
McTighe, J., 49, 110
Means-end strategy, 7–11
Meier, D., 21
Modeling
  in discussion process, 88–89
  in writing process, 73–74, 77
Murray, D., 3

Narrative, 7–11
  classroom transcripts, 8–10
  collaborative narrative with paired
    sentences, 7–11
  means-end strategy, 7–11

paired sentences as writing prompts,
    7–8
  writing prompt, 7–8
National Council of Teachers of English
    (NCTE), xiii, 2–3
Newell, G. E., 95
Newmann, F. M., 17–18, 111, 117
Nussbaum, M. C., 20–21
Nystrand, Martin, ix, 2, 44, 51, 78, 86,
    105–106, 117, 121, 123, 131–132,
    135

Of Mice and Men (Steinbeck), 98, 100
Opening Dialogue (Nystrand), 131–
    132

Paired sentences, 7–11
"The Parents Are Watching" (case),
    31–44
  features of response, 40–41
  language details, 37–38
  large-group discussion, 34–36
  procedures used, 36, 41–43
  product of inquiry procedures, 43–44
  research, 36, 37–38
  sample response, 39–41
  statement of case, 31–33
  writing prompt, 38–39
Participation, 43
Perin, D., xi, 4, 6, 44
"The Playground Bully: A Story in Six
    Episodes" (case), 7–11
Points of view, inquiry into argument,
    14–15
Prewriting activities
  in teaching writing as process, 3
  time devoted to, 2–3
Problem solving
  features of inquiry, 27–28
  framing problems, 26, 30, 32
  problem-based scenarios, 88–90,
    137–140
  problems that resonate with learners,
    29–30

About the Author

Dr. Thomas M. McCann is an associate professor of English at Northern Illinois University, where he contributes to the teacher certification program. He taught English in high schools for 25 years, including seven years working in an alternative high school. He has been a high school English department chair, an assistant principal, and an assistant superintendent. His co-authored books include *In Case You Teach English: An Interactive Casebook for Preservice and Prospective Teachers* (Merrill/Prentice Hall, 2002), *Supporting Beginning English Teachers* (NCTE, 2005), and *Talking in Class* (NCTE, 2006), *The Dynamics of Writing Instruction* (Heinemann, 2010), and *Teaching Matters Most* (Corwin Press, 2012). He co-edited *Reflective Teaching, Reflective Learning* (Heinemann, 2005). NCTE's Conference on English Education awarded him the Richard A. Meade Award for research about the concerns of beginning teachers. He also received the Paul and Kate Farmer Award from NCTE for his writing for the *English Journal*.